LIBERTY
One man's quest for sovereignty in an unrealized democracy

MH Kisner

MH Kisner

Copyright © 2012 by MH Kisner. All rights reserved. Printed in the United States of America. No part of this book may be used or reproduced in any manner whatsoever without written permission of the author except in the case of brief quotations embodied in critical articles or reviews.

ISBN: 978-0-9845605-4-7

Cover Design and Book Design By: Lisa Corcoran

Cover Photograph By: MH Kisner

May 2012 Print On Demand By:
Lightning Source, INC., U.S.
246 Heil Quaker Blvd.
La Vergne, TN 37086 USA

Table of Contents

Prologue ix
Karma...1
An Inquiry Into Applied Values 7
The Tao of Joe 13
Baggage and Bobblehead University..21
Ontology is the Elixir..28
Mormonism & Me 34
Lincoln Liberty and Love 46
Case Study in American Education and Democracy 57
Pushing Boundaries in Law Enforcement & Quantum Physics ...64
The Great American Deception 71
On Not Taking Care of Business 80
Our Long and Windy Road...91
Roadside Reflections..100
Candybars Kill Democracy...114
God's Grace, White "T's", and the Voices in My Head.............120
Bibliography 125
HERMES LETTERS 31, 45, 60, 90, 115, 118, 121, 134

Prologue

High above the clouds, encapsulated in ephemeral mist lies a mythical and mystical civilization. This civilization is blanketed with a dense fog of confusion that separates our world from theirs. It is here, high above mortal man and the pedestrian where I met Phaedrus. Phaedrus was the harbinger of insanity for Robert Pirsig. Phaedrus is not malevolent, not really. In this instance insanity is symptomatic of being intimately aware of what *can be* without fully accepting *what is*.

When a person visits this lofty sphere and peers around the fog of confusion, eventually they will come face-to-face with more contemporary and familiar apparitions. These specters are doomed to haunt humanity for all time, wandering in and out of individual and collective consciousness. America's founding father's bivouac within these Elysian Fields. Gandhi, Lincoln, and Joan-of-Arc all share the same space.

It is here in the mystical realm where what *is,* is confronted with what *can be*. This is where angels fear to tread. This is where laymen become insane men if they are not prepared to accept, to give-in, give-up, and partially die at the altar of what is.

Wrapping one's mind around what is, and defining what truly can be, can be daunting. After all, isn't perspective everything? What and how do we perceive? This line of thinking is innocuous and nefarious. Subtly, your mind will trick you into throwing dagger-like questions under the auspices of finding clarity. Conversely, clarity is much simpler. Clarity doesn't ask questions, or give answers. Clarity is a perpetual outcome infinitely available to all those who just accept what is.

Clarity doesn't ask why a person is homeless. Clarity doesn't ask how social injustice is perpetuated in the greatest country on earth. Clarity won't be found within a flat-tax proposal, or wide-sweeping healthcare reform. Clarity quietly whispers… there are homeless, hungry, sick, oppressed and otherwise disenfranchised citizens. I think very few people hear the voice of clarity. Lasting solutions rarely sprout from people or policies that haven't embraced clarity. Good intentions and great effort don't always equal lasting change. Clarity, understanding, and accepting what is can be a cornerstone for lasting change.

I have visited and sojourned with the aforementioned apparitions much too long! I have pitched my tent around their eerie and mesmerizing circle of light. Their ephemeral and soothing voices inculcated me with ambrosia that is *only* fit for the gods, wreaking havoc and insanity upon a person that has not fully accepted what is. Here is their story and mine, offered with various shades of clarity.

Clarity came to me as I read the last page of *Arrowsmith* by Sinclair Lewis. Sinclair paints the trajectory of a handful of people's lives. One character lives a life of religious piety and pride. Another character lives a life of academic accomplishment. Each character is shown living their choice life on the last page of *Arrowsmith*. Each choice in their lives became a link in the long chain of life. The sum total of their existence could be found in their life choices, the priorities and pathways that they sought after.

Sinclair Lewis' characters illuminated what I could expect by following similar paths in my life. Should I pursue a life of conventional Christian service in a local church, the end of my life would probably look like one of Sinclair Lewis' characters. Who am I and what do I choose on a daily basis? How do I come to terms with the ghosts of American Liberty which bare down upon my conscious in the most unlikely places such as the check out at the grocery? What matters? What do I leave in my life and what do I leave out? What legacy do we leave behind us on the trail to freedom and liberty, just as the founding fathers, revolutionaries, and soldiers of yesteryear have done? Each of us must answer these questions in our own way. How we interpret these conundrums, how we live our lives determines what is found upon the final pages of our lives. What we live for and stand up for is what is found on the beginning pages of our progeny's lives. In the quiet recesses of your mind can be heard your own daemons and demons calling you to action. Leading you to your own middle ground of clarity and confusion.

Karma

> Karma is what is.
> J. Clavelle, *Shogun*.

Bad Karma: A Quilt-Work of Life Experiences and Reflections

One inch more, God help me one inch more.

CRACK!!! Jacob's steel fist pummeled my head like lightning. He had been at it for at least an hour and I knew that once he started, he would continue like a well-oiled machine for hours. THUD!!! My head bounced off the squalor ladened living room floor. My arms are pinned by his massive body; he has this down to an art form.

No shame in his heart, no mercy in his mind. CRACK-THUD! Blood oozes from my nose, my lip, and the skin above my eye. Hell, I am bleeding everywhere. Like Christ; blood seems to ooze from every pore in my body. And in my heart and mind I go to Christ.

My soul repeats a mantra: CRACK-THUD blessed be the meek for they shall inherit the CRACK-THUD earth. Blessed are the pure in heart for they shall CRACK-THUD see God. Blessed are the peacemakers for they shall CRACK-CRACK-THUD be called the children of God. And the pain is gone.

He's over me again; I make a feeble attempt to stand up. WOSH-THUMP. My bruised-bloody head wobbles. I am resigned. "Yes Jacob, you are right, I am nothing." Maybe I know he is right. two hours and fourteen minutes until mom comes home. It won't be long now. WOOSH-CRACK. Eons pass and Jacob throws in the towel. I take the light blue towel that he found under the sink and wipe up my blood off from the floor. His cat eyes and stertorous breathing indicate a sense of self-satisfaction. He starts to pace like a beast from the jungle. "Tell mom that you started it, that you wouldn't leave me alone, and that I just defended myself. Oh ya, go upstairs and put on a long sleeve shirt." Yes, Jacob. He ain't heavy, he's my brother. We both knew that she would not believe me but it didn't matter, she wouldn't do anything.

It takes exactly seven minutes for mom to walk home from the factory. She would be home in 3 minutes. I try to control myself as the flood of pain overcomes my short stout body. My head throbs and then abates as my soul rips apart like a flimsy cloth. I can barely stand as the warm salty streams of tears waterfall from my cheeks. I reel into the bathroom, not willing to give Jacob the satisfaction of truly beating me and taking away my dignity. The front door opens, mom is home. Jacob is upstairs in his dark cavernous lair-like bedroom, waiting, listening. Hurriedly, I reach for mom to giver her a hug, not making eye contact for then she would know. She still has on her bohemian winter coat and fuzzy snow boots. Half of her head is covered with a crocheted purple ear warmer. She made it herself. Her dumpy, short and stout frame is weighed down. Weighed down with grief that I, a ten year old have, shared with her.

I know that she does not have room upon her shoulders for my burden. She has been crying too. I looked up into her hazel green eyes and ask, "What's wrong, mom?" Far from my mind was my own ordeal from today. Mom saw on my face, that which I could not see. She felt what I could no longer feel. The concern, disappointment and angst from my travails flashed upon her face in an instant. And she wept. No longer able to deal with life, with Jacob, with me or our older sister Jennifer who disappeared last week. She wept, and I cowered in the furthest corner that I could find.

We scavenged on our own that night for supper (like most nights). A can of soup, a sandwich; whatever we could find. Darkness had fallen upon our home and enshrouded us without us knowing it. Darkness covered our small hamlet. Only a few streetlights cut through the cold snowy night. Small quaint homes with festive Christmas lights in their windows dotted the surrounding hills. Far away, I knew that cities were busy, high rises towered like lighthouses. Homeless people sat around barrels of fire. But here, here on this dead-end road, in an obscure upstate New York farming town, it was cold and dark. Jennifer turned up in Chicago, with a drug-dealer. We brought her home.

I had spirituality knocked into me at an early age. There was no other refuge, no other safe harbor then the prayers that I sent daily from my heart and lips skyward.

From John Denver's *Peace Poem*:

There's a name for war and killing
there's a name for giving in
when you know another answer
for me the name is sin
but there's still time to turn around
and make all hatred cease
and give another name to living
and we could call it peace

Peace was my primary objective for over 30 years of life. I think peace is still the greatest objective to aim for. However, not many people are seeking peace, inclusive of the clerics, congregation goers, or any other person professing to walk under the banner of peace.

What gets most people going is things…things…and more things. The lingua franca for everyday life is things. Cars, houses, money, toys, and even services like vacations are all things people strive for…it is inescapable; it makes our day. However much of the Judeo-Christian culture vilifies living a life of surplus. And I can see the point. It's taken me a long time along my own journey to understand that surplus, and people with some surplus aren't the core issue. I think there is enough for everyone to have some surplus.

Surplus along with tyranny of the have-nots is the discriminating factor. This failed system of capitalism, or socialism, or whatever kind of economy is the demon that has whipped the masses. This is the silent war that has never been fought in America. The upper class has systematically destroyed the American dream; the dream of life, liberty and the pursuit of happiness.

Life is the act of living one's dream. A dream to be an independent candle-maker, to publish a modest newspaper, to obtain a college education or whatever dream one can dream. Liberty is the ability to access legal rights and remedies with an equitable sense of blind justice. A blind justice that does not capitulate to another based upon race, socio-economic status, nepotism, or any other form of bias. Pursuit of happiness is the ability and opportunity to spend restive and quality time with family (however you define family). For only in a family (a self-identified tribe) can one find happiness. Fleeting moments of happiness can be found by one's self, or in the company of others, yet without the backdrop of a sense of *belonging* to a *family*… everything else is empty.

One of the greatest obstacles to broach when considering peace is a triangle of discernment: Ultimate Utopian peace, chaos & conflict, or a more nebulous state of pockets of peace. There are some that smirk and chide when the term peace is invoked. To them, granola-loving hippies is probably their first image. Chaos and conflict are considered diametrically opposed to peace, yet there is still an opportunity for peace, and peaceful ends. Peace pockets are usually the most overlooked and least considered. Many cultures, and subcultures successfully live in harmony with little or no conflict. Should conflict arise within these peaceful cultures there is a rational (often democratic) process to arrange peaceful results from it. Peace is an option, an overlooked option.

I wasn't entirely alone in my suffering. On Sundays Patti-Ann, a childless lady yearning for motherhood, gave me a lift into church. We sat in the same pew, I think she held me during services. Later, more people came to my rescue albeit temporary, fleeting, and oft-times shallow. However, there was always one silent and real person that I could turn to, someone whose affection had no bounds, my grandfather. I don't ever remember him saying "I love you, I believe in you, or I am proud of you." Yet, I always felt it.

At disconsolate times I would travel to a nearby woodland. Since disconsolation and I were bedmates, I went to the woods often, almost daily. At times I felt very alone in the woods. Metaphorically, I would lick my wounds. I would pray and search. My searches led me far and wide, and always inside of myself. At times I felt a loving presence. In deep snowstorms, I would traverse field, stream, and dark forests hunting for peace, tranquility, and succor. I was 7 years old, a babe…and the wilderness was my maternal breast. Maybe God was there, a benevolent angel, or perhaps Mother Mary or Christ. It's a fanciful thought.

As stoically as I attempted to heft this load, a rare incident of weakness occurred when I was in third grade on the playground. On our school playground was a row of tractor tires half imbedded in the soil.

AWAKENED

In an old tractor tire
Is where I found my home
I nestled and I cuddled in arms all alone.

My soul was in a whirlpool
Headed down, down the drain.
In my arms was me,
A man in miniature.

Years have passed and my tire is still there.
Miles down the road, stages gone with the wind.
And here I am, an evicted soul
Exploring "The Shadow" and "Love."

It was so obvious, why didn't I notice?
Because I was not me.
I float in pools and bubbles of illusion,
living my life as if my lies
could persuade me to believe.

Believe me to be one I am not.
And others to be those they are not
But how I would have them to be.
AWAKENED.

Being awake is over-rated. Sleep is much more pleasant. *"Maybe I am a butterfly dreaming that I am human, or maybe I really am a human that dreamt of being a happy butterfly."* -Master Zhuang. Have you ever noticed that being awake and aware takes a lot of energy and effort? However when we do find rest and sleep this process is effortless? The more effort we exert, the more resistance we find. Consider doing without doing, an autopilot of sorts, the zone, and the effortless place of real accomplishment. This knack may help you when you are out of gas.

I believe in Karma.

I believe that sometimes the quickest path to your destination is often found in the opposite direction of your goal.

I believe that good is relative but not all relatives are good.

MH Kisner

An Inquiry Into *Applied* Values

Robert Pirsig delves into a theoretical inquiry of values in his seminal work Zen and the Art of Motorcycle Maintenance (ZAMM).

Values are the lens through which we perceive all things. From motorcycles to large social ills, using one of Robert Pirsig's scalpels is fundamental to identifying strengths and weaknesses within a system, an item, or a person. I have a 1982 Honda 750 CBK motorcycle. It works for me. It has its flaws, things that I could and should improve. Why should I improve or work on this motorcycle? It is legal and gets me down the road. Because the motorcycle is 30 years old with that many years of wear and tear, cosmetic and functional chores arise that could prolong its life.

Pirsig would jump-to, roll up his sleeves and fix it, to make it mirror the ideal. I on the other hand have a different heuristic. Like Pirsig I weigh my personal relationship to this machine, maybe even more than Pirsig would with a motorcycle. Some indigenous tribes believe that items have a spirit of their own, something akin to sentience. I happen to believe that all things are vibrating and connected, and quantum physics is supporting this theory. So my train of thought departs from Pirsig's. My acumen begs me to ask the following questions of my motorcycle, and our relationship: Where on the continuum of time-space have we met and where will we depart? What is the purpose or meaning of the motorcycle in my life at this point? Why should I hold onto it, fix it, or get rid of it? And of course the more pedestrian questions that coalesce around utilitarian equations, If I put $xx into the motorcycle will I get $xx out of it? Etc.

What a mind trip all of this is! Truly there are no guarantees in life, however the process is nearly compulsory. We are emotional creatures. We invest emotionally into the people, places and things in our life, even those items that are not considered heirloom quality. We imprint items with cathexis. Our lives are teaming with emotional investment. In ancient times, it is well accepted that mankind was aware of their role in life; the elements and items around them were invested and at times divested of emotional energy. Mankind was intimate with his immediate environs. In ancient times a native's coup stick was not only a latent icon of himself, the coup stick was a salient manifestation of his entirety. One's coup stick or personal affect was imbued with the owner's energy and the energy of deities, elementals, and the energy of one's milieu.

It can be argued that a similar relationship occurs within our modern lives, just more subconsciously than our predecessors. Words and actions have meanings. Believe half of what you hear and less of what you see is a wonderful axiom. As we have entered a world of exacting political correctness, our speech has become diluted and nearly meaningless. Our actions are our manifestos. We *value* non-confrontational language. We value fitting in, conformity, and congeniality. Yet our actions speak a different language. Our actions speak of divisive, self-centered lifestyles, and a primal dog-eat-dog modus operandi. I have been aware of the disparity of interpersonal, local, and national values as it is spoken, and then as it has been applied throughout my life, truly this is a baneful curse. It is a baneful curse to be aware of the impediments to democracy and simultaneously be unable to affect change due to one's financial station in life. The common reflex is to point to a few bright stars that outshone their station in life. Yet, even Ghandi was an educated lawyer. Dr. Martin Luther King Jr. came from a middle-class family and was well educated. Outshining one's station in life is a miracle, a statistical phenomenon, and a rare cosmic event unto itself.

A curse is a real and sure thing. Just as a blessing is a real process. Many Christians don't believe in curses, nor their function in modern life. It seems much easier and orderly for good Christians to grasp onto blessings, being blessed, and the function of blessings in contemporary life. Curses and blessings are two sides of the same coin. Truly you can't bless one, without sending a curse somewhere else. "Lord bless my child that he/she may get into such-and-such prestigious school." This invocation sounds well and good, however consider what happens when your prayer comes true. Would you pray for the same blessing knowing that another deserving candidate got bumped? We are entering a threadbare and tenuous web where all things are connected.

Is it a bad thing to curse something or someone? Does the curse come back to you? Maybe, maybe not. I think if you are prepared to bless one pet project or person, you are well on the road to cursing another project or person. One coin, two sides.

Well, it's all up to God, Divine Providence, or my Creator. It's in God's hands, He decides through divine will. Then why the dickens did you pray for your crummy kid to get into the University anyways? You are trying to curry favor, sweeten the hand of the house-dealer, and affect the outcome of a situation; Magick and voodoo.

In the beginning, we discussed my 1982 motorcycle. *Consciously* deciding the future of a motorcycle is one thing, deciding the fate of our failing nation is another. This is a mammoth concept to contemplate. The decision of our nation's future has probably been decided for us, as we have little to no voice in its day-to-day governance. Fight or flight are our options. Fight? How? With what ammunition and upon what ground? We cannot fight upon the current ground as it is owned, and we are dispossessed. Bring true ideas and ideals of change to a current Republican or Democrat function, and watch yourself be hushed, ignored or laughed out of the room.

Will another Mahatmas Gandhi or Reverend Dr. Martin Luther King surface and lead our nation back into the hands of its true owners –We the people? Will America go the way of Rome? In many ways I suspect that it is. Rome was conquered from within by not truly assimilating its citizens and territories, much like America is devolving now with pockets of ethnicities that share few commonalities. Rome was infected with less than noble, and less than competent leaders; an elite that was dysfunctional, self-serving and out of touch with its countrymen... If this pattern doesn't seem related to America, might I suggest stepping into reality.

LIBERTY

Short of the Rapture arriving, or an alien invasion occur imposing a potent political peaceful regime…America will fall, from within. This is one of the saddest sentences that I could conceive. The pleasure and passion for one's nation runs deep. All that our ancestors lived and fought for lies in the balance.

A gnarly guitar lick reverberates and interrupts my train of thought:

"American woman get away from me…

I don't need your war machines, I don't need your ghetto scenes"

I am told that the woman in this song is the Statue of Liberty, and America. What docs the Statue of Liberty and America stand for? There are staunch American loyalists, if they picked up this book to read they have probably put it down by now. Some loyalists would quip "If you don't like it, leave it." Which truly is a juvenile and uneducated stance. If you don't like it, stay and fight for it to be better! Is a more potent and mature posture.

The right to revolt is a necessary function for any lasting form of democracy. The need to probe basic questions of who are we? Who leads us? And why..why…why are always pertinent in a democracy. Why are we going to war? Why haven't we fixed our infrastructure? Why does our society have socio-economic castes that can be identified by geography, filial composition, etc.

When we fail to allow revolt, we fail to allow democracy.

Riding a motorcycle can be a huge rush like an amusement ride. Riding a motorcycle can be calming, peaceful, and meditative. Riding a motorcycle can be a rush and meditative at the same time. For us that tend to be too cerebral, riding a motorcycle can offer a mental enema, so to speak. Whatever your preconceived notions are about riding a motorcycle, consider changing them, even if you are an avid and veteran rider.

The sum of all life is in its details, and so it is with motorcycling. Face your bike, handlebars in front of you, seat beside you. Gather yourself together, be intentional, and focus. Your helmet is on, your clothing is appropriate and ready. Grab the far handle and squeeze the brake handle. Straddle-up. Kick stand up, *don't screw this up!* Your life is at stake! Taking off with your kickstand down has scuffed up and killed many a person!

Kickstand is up, cut-off switch is on "on." Turn your key on. Get ready here we go! Right thumb pushes the start button. She turned over first try! Listen to her purr…. It's a beautiful noise, felt the power reverberate up your spine, through your body, touching your soul. You're in neutral, give her some gas, and throttle with your right hand. Pull in the clutch lever with your left hand. Left foot taps you into first gear. Slowly let your left hand let go of the clutch, let go and let gas take over. Now's a good time to pray if you're religious. Slowly giving gas with your right hand. The power of your life is finally in your own hands! Give with the gas slowly, take your grip from the clutch slowly. See… Life is a constant action of give and take at the same time.

Your body tugs forward by the power of faith and reason. Roll back and forth a dozen times, giving and taking with the clutch and gas. When you are ready, and only you will know when you are ready, give it gas and take off. Don't worry about stopping…just drive and run out of gas!

Why should you run out of gas? Why not? Running out of gas is instructive. Running out of gas on purpose is easier to hack than running out of gas by accident. In life, we run out of gas at the worst times. When it rains it pours. How do you handle life when you run out of gas enroute to that big job interview? Nothing like being stuck by the side of the road in sleet, rain, or snow and out of gas. Literally, we should have checked the gas first in the above exercise. Metaphorically, there is little in life that you can do when you hit rock bottom, run out of gas, and are proverbially stuck beside the road.

Life is a fickle mistress; love her too much and she'll turn and bite you. Spurn her, and a personal death occurs… a hollow existence of rage, frustration and spite. Ignore life with an added gentle caress on occasion, and things will turn out as best they can, quite mediocre. Some have the whole canvas painted in their life, love and career, success and enjoyment, family and social status. These are the people I loathe with more than a tinge of envy.

I am very lucky in love. I have a wonderful family, great kids, marriage, and stability. No stepchild, babies' daddy issues here. So far, my kids listen and respond to both affection and direction. Over my shoulder is a cursed karmic monkey. It seems that nothing that I do vocationally sticks. Specifically, I raise the ire of most people that come in contact with me. I seriously think there is a mystical component to this problem. On the worst end of the spectrum, I can be engaged, passionate-eager, analytical, creative and energetic all at once. If you have any of these traits, snuff them out. No one likes these traits, no matter how they profess to enjoy working with said people. Be a cog, do without doing, camouflage at all costs.

The Tao Of Joe

Sitting in a diner. The smell of homemade muffins and cookies waft through the air, a sweetness lingers and I am home. McGraw is a small town in upstate New York. If you are thinking of New York City, you are worlds a way from McGraw. McGraw is so small that it does not have a traffic light. The first black college was started in this town circa 1830's. The Underground Railroad piped through this town leaving hidden alcoves in residential basements, tunneling, and stories of main stations such as the Hathaway house abound. The greatest and most awe inspiring artifact left behind from these troubled times is a greater understanding and level of tolerance for people of color, or different ethnicities.

Today there are very few people of color in town. Grace extends to all people. Small acts of kindness: Opening a door, how are you today?, need a ride somewhere? Want help changing that flat tire? This is the quintessential slice of American pie oft-times missing from the hustle and bustle of other cities, worlds apart. Day dreaming in the 50's style diner... staring through a transparent Elvis window sticker to a sleepy main street, sans traffic, sans crime, sans obnoxious and piercing EMS or police sirens' wails. Joe's dream has birthed. Joe's 50's diner is a creation of his own heart and hands, not a Frankenstein. Joe has breathed life into this project much like Galatea's Pygmalion. Galatea was a sculptor that loved his work so much especially his sculpture Pygmalion! Galatea's love for Pygmalion awakened life in an otherwise non-existent form. Joe became a creator in the tradition of a god.

Joe stands maybe 5'1, a diminutive man, bald with a mustache. Joe is a devoted volunteer fireman & paramedic. He doesn't have a career per se. He's done it all. He dj's at local honky-tonks. He dispatches for emergency medical services. Joe does double shifts as a paramedic. Joe is married the second time around with adult children and a four-year-old daughter. Joe is a dreamer. His dreams involve poodle skirts, music from the 1950's and chili sauce. Joe has opened a 50's theme diner, and all his friends have flocked to sample his supper. Joe's first week brought him threefold success, three times the projected sales that he anticipated.

Tom is with me. Tom straight and true like the cedars of Lebanon. Tom is more than a step-dad. He has *always* been there for me. My sons William and Haydn garnish the sides of the table with their cute, quiet and well-behaved ways. Joe has just opened his diner, and we are here to support him.

What can I get for you guys? Joe wakes me from my somnambulism. Tom has been staring at a one-sided menu photocopied on computer paper. So far the menu is very basic. "Hey, you have to start somewhere," Joe tells us. I am thinking Joe has not borrowed one red penny to do this project. I voice within my mind "Good for you Joe!" Jerry Lee Lewis pounds away on a piano right at this moment, maybe he is stuck in the tiny box in the corner we call a radio. I muse still to myself "Didn't he marry his 14 year old cousin? *Good for you Jerry! Good for you!!*"

Burgers, dogs, French fries, a sundry of basic sandwiches, and soup are our choices. By God, I choose soup. "Sorry, we are out of soup," Joe states with a pinch of pride, "We sold out." *Good for you Joe! Good for you!!* I silently muse. Our order is in, Rosa Joe's wife, gathers our menus and goes to work in a kitchen beyond swinging saloon like doors. We holler into the kitchen heckling Rosa our cook.

"Well Tom, we've got a week from today before our road trip, have we missed anything in our planning?" Tom replies with a shrug, "No I guess we'll just take it as it comes. *"Good for you Tom! Good for you Tom!!"* I'm just in that kind of mood. I heft a three ring binder from the floor and hand it to him. Here are our reservations, directions, and phone numbers, the itinerary. I remind him that I hope to camp out most of the ten nights, we need to save money in our budget. The car has had an oil change, and my motorcycle is running great.

I pause to field a question or comment from Tom, of which none is forthcoming. I tried to have this meeting with him a week before at his house however Jacob was there mooching, tying up the computer for hours and hours. At that time I was working with Tom and an atlas where we should camp around Washington D.C. I was looking for a state or national park first, or secondly a small privately owned campground west of Washington D.C.

Jacob travels out of the computer room and tells me we should stay at a KOA campground. Thanks Jacob, we'll look into it I reply gracefully. Ten minutes later Tom and I are narrowing down our prospects for a bivouac near D.C. Jacob again travels out, *"You need to go to a KOA!"* Thank you! I force out from my lungs, we've got it Jacob.. thanks again! My patience is wearing thin. Making reservation phone calls. Jacob resurfaces "You *need* to go to a KOA, trust me Josh I know what I am talking about…I mean it's not like I haven't crossed the country staying at them." Jacob, I really want to take the boys to state and national parks for the history, this our trip and we're doing it our way. Too much tension in the air, I gather my tribe and head for the hills. Now, at Joe's diner…we can breathe deep and work uninterrupted.

Joe slings our grub. *"Hey Joe where you going with that gun in your hand..."* comes to mind in a flash as I see our chum Joe. This is a really nice place Joe! Squinting at Joe for effect and holding my cup of joe close to my chest. Joe tells me a bit of his life history, worked as a mechanic, construction, had this business or that. Joe is a searcher too. A tinge of guilt enters my mind as I formulate my deviant plan to rob Joe. Only half listening to him now, everyone is chowing but me. I hate cold food. Well that's a lie.

We gobble our vittles and send salvos of banter back and forth. The boys are angels. Our plans are set. Will I get caught stealing? Jail time? Will Joe and Rosa hate me? Will Tom be blackballed in the fire department for cavorting with such a shady and unsavory character as myself? We have crossed the Rubicon, no turning back… what is partially done, will be played out fully.

LIBERTY

Night falls, the children are tucked-in and mostly asleep. My dastardly plan is set and I prepare for robbery. The wife has always had a suspicious mind, truly she must know that we can't go on together with suspicious minds. She rifles questions at me, where you going, how long you gonna be gone, why are you going now, on and on. I was honest, mostly. I never said yeah I'm gonna go steal from friends. Honest nearly to the "T", yet my guilt is heavy and I must go.

Adrenaline pumps through my system. I feel almost martial, a knight of sorts as I don riding gear and the coup de grace, a helmet. The effect is complete. I am a knight on a mission. A single piercing beam of light penetrates the oily darkness of the night. I choke my bike. A threatening combustion of noise fills the air. With a throaty and bawdy idle, I slip into gear, a quick stamp with my left foot, first gear with a well timed grab-release of the left hand clutch handle. Off into the night.

Stealth through speed into enemy territory, penetrating dark forests and navigating pocked roads. I park my rumbly beast of burden next to Joe and Rosa's house in an empty car lot. Four cars for sale by appointment only. Nonchalantly dismounting, perusing the street for intel, looking for the enemy, the witness to my debauchery. Someone sitting in the dark on a porch directly across the road. I slip into an even more covert mode. I must pull-off a scheme of deception, the road ahead going out of town has a bend in it, and a cop could easily materialize instantly. A price I must weigh.

Grabbing my helmet in my hand, I march confidently to the front door, and pretend to knock on the door. No one answers, to the next door, no one answers. I drop my do rag, a cloth worn under my helmet, bend over to pick it up scoop my do rag and my kidnapped article into my helmet. Sauntering slowly back to my bike, heart racing. What did the porch sitter see? Will the sheriff come now and question me? Is someone calling the cops? Did Joe and Rosa's light go on? I stow my stolen booty into my oversized saddlebag. Regulators mount up!

I head home still tweaked on adrenaline. The house is quiet and I begin interrogating my captive, a garden gnome named Hermes Trismegistus (Hermes Thrice Great). We battle it out in spades both staring at each other, unrelenting. Not intimidated by his cool as a clam composure, with furrowed brow I sling incrminating questions his way. At first Hermes just stares blankly at me, mirthful, teasing me with his secrets. Time rolls off the clock like water on a wheel. Hermes is now ready. I am the Thrice Great Hermes, keeper of knowledge, I am the tao (divine way) of all ideas, I am keeper of mysteries and master of magic. And modest at that I add telepathically after his declaration. Yes, that was a modest statement because deep and true are my ways, eons pass of enlightened men and women searching my ways yet and mankind has experienced very little of my bounty.

Well that will change right now! I counter with feigned moxy. Silence pervaded our time and filled our shared space as if silence was his message, silence owned the moment and then another moment until a seemingly endless chain of moments was ruled by silence. Was Hermes telling me that silence is the sum total of all and nothing? Or is silence the device to throw me off the right track…to hedge from devulging rich gems of arcane knowledge; panaceas.

Silence continued to tyranize the evening until Hermes broke his quiet vigil "What you seek you have, what you know will be unknown again and again, where you are going you have gone, all things come to those who wait, sleep is the salve of mystics, comedians, and all people…especially seekers. Your task now is to sleep and all will be revealed, one day at a time. One thought, one word, one step will define your path and answer all." Reluctantly, I went to the couch, my place of sleep, and dug under my covers. Sleep came and sleep went, morning brought another day and yet I didn't feel closer to my goal.

The following days were filled with excitement and fiduciary tasks in preparation for our roadtrip. I would travel by motorcycle, whilst my wife Stephanie, and sons William and Haydn, and Tom would follow behind me in the family car. In between the frenetic packing, list making, supply shopping and day to day rhythm, I would return to my captive Hermes and again begin the drill:

LIBERTY

Tell me what you know! And again time rolls off the clock like water on a wheel. Silence and waiting fill the space, finally: *I am the Thrice Great Hermes, keeper of knowledge, I am the tao (divine way) of all ideas, I am keeper of mysteries and master of magic.*

Many times within a day, followed by many days and many ways of rephrasing my plea, Hermes only offered one set of words: *I am the Thrice Great Hermes, keeper of knowledge, I am the tao (divine way) of all ideas, I am keeper of mysteries and master of magic.*

Until and at last, after positing my question for the gazillionth time and waiting for a reply, which by now I memorized with a putrid distaste for the familiar…Hermes offered new words, yet old ideas:

Begin with nothing, a circular round, empty, hollow and all things lie outside of its nothingness. Nothing is the reflection of everything. Everything is nothing, and nothing (no-thing) is everything. *Righhht*…I counter telepathically. If nothing is everything…then what is this pencil…Nothing and everything, Hermes replied.

August 8, 2011

Dear Joe and Rosa,

Watching cars come and go has made me lonely for the open road. I've hitched a ride with a friendly band of carnival gypsies (carnies). I'll send a note, a postcard now and then, and I promise to be back before school starts!

Please listen to *Shooting Star,* by Bad Company, and think fondly of me.

Forever Yours,

Hermes Trismegistus (AKA Hermes)

Ps. Google my name.

Psss…. Here is some $ to hold my place in the front yard…. The other gnomes are mean to me! THOSE B@$TARDS!!

LIBERTY

It sounded like mumbo jumbo to me, another evasive device to not really answer my question. Yet I was quickly reminded of a few theories within quantum physics that suggest that all things are connected at subatomic level. Living and non-living things co-exist and vibrate at separate yet connected frequencies within an energetic field or fields. I easily percieve that I am a male rendition of Alice falling through a rabbit hole. With my head spinning, I'm the one that demands silence for a change.

I believe *"A man hears all that he wants to hear and disregards the rest."*- Paul Simon

MH Kisner

Baggage And Bobblehead University

Packing our bags and man do I have a lot of baggage! Ideas and concerns swirl through my thoughts, trying to grab one by the tail, capture it, and file it away properly is daunting. What is my priority? What specific goals do I have? How do I organize and express what this journey is all about? How do I make my words meaningful for myself and others? I can understand others but can I be understood by others effectively through this chain of words and sentences that is a book?

I am taking a 2003 white Suzuki Intruder VL800. The license plate spells LIBERTY, saddlebags, highway bars, half size sissy bar, and a windshield make my bike an impressive image. I have named my steel white steed Spirit. I will travel with Spirit. I have only two complaints regarding this bike. One complaint has been addressed, the other persists. Within Spirit's infancy, less than 5500 miles, someone changed the original carberator jets out for smaller ones creating a machine that loped, coughed and otherwise dogged-out. The solution was easy, replace the jets for larger ones. Problem solved.

The second problem is a malfunction with the stereo. Without notice or prompting, the stereo comes on, on its own. At times the signal is strong and music will blare without warning. At times, the signal seems weak, a faint whisper flits and lingers in the air. Some problems are not meant to be solved. Much of life we must accept as a matter of course with noble sanguinity.

Traveling is really no easy task. So much preparation or groundwork goes into a simple short-run, let alone a lengthy expedition. In one sense all of your life's experiences have led you to this point. All of your formal and informal education is now mustered today, for today's wear and tear. Your starting point is always here and now summed up with all that has been in your life.

Packing, unpacking, and repacking your bags is a life skill, one of the hardest to master. Defining what one needs on the road ahead, a path yet untraveled is paramount for a successful foray. Many of us pack what we we used yesterday, stuff that was decided for us and given to us by others. We carry baggage that isn't our own. It's ours because we accept it, and shoulder it without questioning it nor the person(s) that gave it to us. I have a boon of questions regarding the baggage that I shoulder now.

I have to know what I am taking with me on this trip and what baggage I will return with. What a fantastic and over simplified metaphor this baggage concept is! Like a feel good movie ending, just dropping our baggage is jejune, sophomoric and utterly farsical! Yet maybe this baggage metaphor is a start, a step in the right direction, no warranties or panaceas promised.

A crossroads lies before us: say three unknown paths. We know what lies behind us, at times too intimately. With only a broken compass and a loathesome taste in our mouths of what currently is, any path any direction will do! Dear God, just don't let it be more of the same!

Time marches on as it always does. The morning of truth has arrived. We have installed a soft car top carrier on our blue Jeep Laredo. The kids are buckled, and we proceed on the first 8 miles of our journey. To Gramma's house we go. Grandpa Tom is ready for us and the boys are filled with more excitement than what their little four and six year old bodies can handle. Ergo, grandpa and I rough-house with them to get some energy out.

The boys are tamed, grandpa's personal effects are added to the growing bulge of the car top carrier. Something electric happens, a moment of knowing, of quietude that often occurs right before momentous action. Our goodbyes to Grandma, my mom, are said. The boys are belted. I slowly and thoughtfully prepare. American flag do rag first, placed right above my brow the same spot each time, byproduct of my OCD (obsessive compulsive) nature. Tuck my shirt behind my suspenders, dangling above my butt. Swinging my full face helmet with speed above my head and lowering it over my ears slowly. Life is a stage. Sunglasses, notched my mirror tinted visor, aha…I can see you…you can't see me.

Standing next to my stead I grab the clutch handle and pop my right leg over this beast in a hurry as if it would bolt out from underneath me had I acted otherwise. Settle in, check the mirrors. KaPow! The engine starts with a fierce and piercing chop. Check the throttle…rev it. Let it slip, slap it hard and watch the birds in the trees and powerlines fly. Head for the hills, it's time. First gear and 50 miles faster than money in a politician's pocket.

Hermes has made my saddlebag into a sidecar. Silent and content, Hermes is quiet. I am filled with noise, the internal noise that makes one edgy, anxious. Side mirror, Tom is just pulling out of the driveway loping along. I am at the end of the road, stop sign. Spirit, Hermes and I are ready to go, to do, to become. We are ready to be Pygmalion *or* Galatea. Go south young man, go south. Spirit points south, a swift spin onto Interstate 81 south.

The first hour is filled with hand signals and waves. The boys haven't seen me on motorcyle from this view, 80 mph. Life is good, and then it rains. Man I hope it doesn't rain the whole trip! I'll be fine but the wife will crumble and then we will argue, and argue, and argue. Clipping along, humming and chopping, Hermes, Spirit and I are ready for adventure.

After an hour of travel, we are at the Pennsylvania border. Three hundred plus or minus miles to travel, much time to think, to not think, to think about thinking and not thinking. No matter how you are wired, whether you are a deep thinker, or creative, or anaylitical, or the basic type that has found true harmony in life and realize that thinking doesn't pay much, thinking and non-thinking are alike. People process things, and categorize things, and develop their own awareness (knowledge sets) of their environs. This processed stuff becomes our own philosophy in life, our modis operandi, our life heuristic. We are all philosophers with our own philosophies. My philosophy in life: I will gain experience, common sense knowledge, street smarts, I will understand the pedestrian as well as the arcane, *I will know and be the tao,* even if I have to crack the nut of life, or caress her till she unfolds passionately in my grasp. Funny how things and money factor into my heuristic only peripherally, there's a thinker.

Chopping and humming, in Pennsylvania headed to the land of cotton. *Well times are getting tough for you little girl, I've been humming and a strumming all over God's world.* Great, I think with a splash of chagrin, the motorcycle's stereo popped on, spouting glam rock from the 80's, The Great White... *my my my, once bitten twice shy babe!* I thump on the gas tank, and looking down, around and confused I shake my head. What makes us think that a thump will fix a problem like this? It's like ducking in the rain. Very illogical. Nothing to be done at 90 mph so I resign myself with sanguinity to my fate. I listen submissively to this tune played over and over on the radio, and finally a litany of other 80' glam rock. It is what it is.

Sometimes life goes from bad to worse, to even worse yet. One March day EMS responders scurried above my naked chest in an Elementary School nurse's office. The Assistant Principal and the Principal lurked unwelcomingly in the door jam. My heart pounded at an unfathomable pace... Nearly exploding within my chest. I blacked out.

I awoke to being loaded into an ambulance on a gurney. I remember nearly every waking moment at the local hospital, INOVA outside of D.C. It's hinky how memory works. I can remember very little of today or yesterday. Yet details of moments like this are indelible. Days like this, my cardiac event can be considered good only as it pales in comparison to other days.

I learned something that day, I just don't know what. I've always been for learning. However, some lessons are very costly for the wallet, body, and soul. Earning one's doctorate is often considered the epitome of learning and of having learned, at least in that surreal world we call academia.

I enrolled in a doctoral program about this time. To protect the guilty, the clueless, and nearly useless, I'll call that university Bobblehead. Bobblehead University is a real place, a private four-year university south of the Mason-Dixon line. I learned so very much at Bobblehead U., unfortunately, I learned very *little* by way of academic arts. I learned *very* little research, writing or critical thinking at this university. Some lessons are very costly for the wallet, body, and soul.

The place was Virginia. The time was shortly after the Virginia Tech massacre. I neither condemn nor condone the actions of rogue shooters like this, people "going postal," examples of the Columbine Effect. In my estimation, these people and incidents are communicating to us, to society at-large. Are we listening? This is just one point where I screwed-up at Bobblehead U.

Most people just condemn such gunman as crazy. This could be true, then again, maybe not. All things happen in context with the world around them. The founding fathers were "crazy," suffragettes, slaves, and all bondsmen have been condemned as crazy. My doctoral student candidates did not like the lines of which I was thinking along. Ergo, I must be crazy too.

I'm a magnet for disaster. I am the Statue of Liberty:

"Give me your tired, your poor,
Your huddled masses yearning to breathe free,
The wretched refuse of your teeming shore.
Send these, the homeless, tempest-tost to me,…"

Emma Lazarus-1883

The hurt and wounded flock to me. I am *the* Clara Barton of emotional wounds, I am James Taylor's *Handyman*. And so it was that many of my doctoral cohorts came to me for emotional succor, advice, and an emotional place for reprieve. "I've never told anyone this before…not

LIBERTY

even my husband but..." or "I am really unprepared for this assignment, can you help me?" "I have an extra house on the market... I don't know how I should proceed..." "My 10 year old daughter is having problems making friends at school...can you drive 65 miles up here, meet her and encourage her?"

I never shirked this extra load. I have problems of my own, I was a young dad with important priorities to place my efforts. Helping rarely helps. Nothing is more addictive and pernicious than hope, the belief in humanity, the higher ideals of social conscious. The more you help someone, the more *intimately* you help them, the more they will resent you. An unsavory axiom.

Jealousy is an endemic disease among those with strong egos. A strong ego can be viewed as one that believes in their own might, their own way, and is inflexible.. Being unwilling to see the forest through the trees is a person with a strong ego. Many of the American elite, and even within the middle class have strong egos intact. Work works for me, therefore work should work for the poor. Within this doctoral program were students who have led narrow lives. As one student succinctly put it "I've read very few books... I read only one magazine; Sports Illustrated and especially one issue (alluding to their bathing suit issue)." This doctoral student is an assistant principal, a strong advocate for education. He called me a piece of shit.

During a breakout session we were given the scenario of an accounting error by a normally trustworthy friend-work associate. I suggest that we find the right policy "loophole" to tide our fiscal reporting until the next reporting session until a further audit was done to determine culpability. For that I am a "piece of shit." Thank you Mr. Assistant Principal... just be nice to my children during the day, because in your eyes... they are?

During another focus group, we were separated men here, women there, and given the challenge of discussing the Martha Stewart scandal. Much of our group time was engrossed with the guys voicing their decision to strip search, and full body cavity search wayward Martha, of which I voiced my desire to not be any part of that, rather let's focus on the assignment. My GPA was above 3.8, neither a slouch nor a dunce.

I was not without sin. I raised my hand and participated too much. Think Horshack from *Welcome Back Kotter,* no one likes an overly vocal participant. I wasn't overbearing and demanding with my ideas. However, I was original. I quoted much from classical works much to the chagrin of my Sports-Illustrated counterparts. My greatest faux pas was in year two of our studies. Our group was kinda nonchalant. Much of our integral and side discussions revolved around booze. We went out for drinks as a group, treated by the professor/department chair. Our class was in a bar one evening. One student queried the group for advice on how to entertain her grandson, one student replied "Drink heavily!"

One summer evening, after working all day outside in the summer heat. I brought a beer to class in a paper bag and drank one beer. That was stupid of me, I took the chance thinking that if anyone was offended they would tell me, I'd get a warning…a slap on the hand and go on my merry way.

My second infraction was mourning the death of my 17-year-old niece. I was very close to her, I babysat her nearly everyday from age one to five years old. She passed in a freak car accident. I was stunned, and hurt. I came back to the classes tired, worn down, my dress was more casual, my hair spiked. I was more reserved and less participatory. Being a pack of wolves, they used this marked change to make a fatal blow at my credibility.

One night I asked to be excused from class and received permission from the instructor who was also the department chair. He used that class session to discuss any and all grievances against me, real or imagined. No one, not a single soul that I helped with friend-like counseling spoke up and said "Hey, I think we shouldn't talk behind his back… let's give him a chance." In my email the next morning was a dossier of these comments, and a memo from the professor withdrawing me from the courses I was currently enrolled in. I must stop in and see campus security before returning to the building. I learned something that day, I just don't know what it is.

Ontology Is The Elixir

Many people from Asia are said not to measure time by hours and days, but by generations of children, dynasties. Few people realize that if you maliciously attack one's ability to earn, to build equity, you are effecting that person's children, and grandchildren. Truly the root word of livelihood is live or life. You destroy one's livelihood and you destroy their life. This is fair game in capitalism. We do not make the connection or separation of this type of warfare, one that is more certain than a literal death. Afterall, children and grandchildren benefit from one's life earnings and lifestyle, whilst losing out should their parent's life be blunted, or decimated. Food for thought.

The heat is nearly too much. We've left the steep mountains of northern Pennsylvania behind us. Traveling through Harrisburg, the state capitol at a nice clip, Over a vast bridge expanding over the Susquehanna, yachts and commercial boats are moored at an island and willy-nilly at one piling or another. I failed to put sunscreen on, and I will pay dearly for it. The road becomes flat and straight, the sun does not relent. We're headed to Patapsco State Valley State Park in Maryland.

Hermes rides nobly in my saddlebag turned sidecar. We pull over for gas and to stretch. The boys want drinks. I reposition the weight from the saddlebag hanging over the exhaust pipes to the other side. The saddlebag was sitting on the pipes, slowly eating away at the fine leather and leaving a mark on the pipes, not good. I enjoy riding motorcycle so much! Its so liberating, one must be alert at all times. Paradoxically, riding motorcycle is very meditative for me.

We leave Interstate 81 and skirt east in harried and more populated highways. As the past four hours were filled with the monotonous hum and strum of straight highway, our driving rhythm is now more staccato, hurry up slow down, merge, enter a new highway, leave an old one.

Motorcyclists need to be seen. So many drivers of cars and trucks fail to see a motorcyclist. Riding motorcycle can be thrifty; very inexpensive insurance at $75 a year, great gas mileage about three hundred miles on a full tank of four gallons. Riding motorcycle can be very expensive if you don't keep it rubber side down. Motorcyclists need to keep a relaxed focus, Zen.

We chose Patapsco State Valley State park as it was close to D.C. After five hours of being on the road in sweaty blistering heat, we hang left after penetrating a small town. We are now traveling down a shaded avenue with pricey Victorian homes adorning each side of the road. This byway is broken up with speed bumps every 1000 yards or so. I'm on "E" and don't know if my loyal steed will make it to the campsite and back to gas. Tom and I register at the camp booth guarding ingress and egress. My do rag, is dripping with sweat I hang it from my handlebars. The boys are well behaved, I decide to be naughty and get them riled up with kisses, raspberries, and bodily noises that moms and wives loathe so much.

Into the camp we go deer greet us in adjacent meadows by peering and pausing above their wild grass fare. We all take note that there is a huge playground. I make a solemn vow to myself that I will take the boys to it tonight no matter how tired, hungry, thirsty I am after setting up camp. Steph climbs on top of the jeep to make an incision with her hands into the goiter like car top carrier. Sitting on top of the car, she looks so special! One tent up, then another, I will sleep sans tent or air mattress. Their beds are made. Now for food, a consensus is made that we need to pick up a few items, and I must bring the motorcycle for gas.

On the road again, detours in this small town, we skirt around town searching for the grocer. A few wrong turns and then losing each other in the oversized parking lot that hosts five or more large stores. I small talk with the young and nubile clerk, a gorgeous vahine. My wife hates it when I small talk with those easy around the eyes. Almost fourteen years of marriage, and I have not cheated on her…nor will I, I think.

LIBERTY

On the road again, Gas for my chopper, back to the camp. The boys and I walk to the playground. I sit down and rest feeling more than a bit guilty for not being up playing with them. Tom and Steph join us, they brought the car and water for me. After about 20 ounces of cold water and I am up for my regular impish antics. I chase down the boys, and let them chase me. We've played this game a few times a day for a couple of years now, we know our parts well, and we never tire of the script. Tom joins in the mix. Good ole' faithful Tom, I can trust him with anything. He is very good with the boys and loves them entirely. The boys adore their grandfather. It's time for me to rest again.

With only a few interruptions from Steph, I travel to those high places, which Pirsig alluded to. At times I wish Steph would join me here. However I know it's not her nature to travel this way. Deep down, I relish the aloneness and loneliness that such travels proffer me. The world around me fades, and I am lost in haze. Demons and Daemons gather around me.

The elixir is ontology, the study of identifying knowing and being. What things exist without names? If we label something as X, does our labeling it make it true? The answer is truly yes, no, and maybe. We have a tendency to view things only in the moment, not in the future, and rarely from the past. If there was an island of purple people, would they be less than human? Would we bond them to slavery or otherwise exploit them? Because in the past, people of African descent, Irish, Asian, and at times German descent were thus so treated right here in our own country. The oppressors were more than comfortable in classifying these denizens as less than human and in some instances without souls. In this instance there seems to be more than one reality. There is a societal reality and a humane reality. The societal reality begged for bondage. The humane reality demanded freedom. If this is so, what societal realities are we cleaving to now that fail to meet the humane reality?

All of this mulling reminds me of a dark time of my past in the doctoral program. One female and elitist professor had expressed ambivalence regarding the influx of Latino folks in America. She acknowledged that she relied upon this populace for housekeeping and yard work, yet resented the change in landscape of the country. In an instant I recalled two conversations: one with this professor and another with the department chair. I mentioned to the first professor that I had my hands full with yard work… and she quipped "yard work!? That's for the Mexicans." The second comment from the department chair was just as hurtful. I volunteered for a quality improvement committee. I asked the department chair why I had not heard back from the committee… he stated via email that "I probably wasn't of the right race."

Back on the playground watching my boys I let out a painful cough and awkward chortle. Not out of humor, but out of pain. The other parents looked at me and returned their attention to their children. Little did they know. Back to ontological musing. We create what we believe. Our act of believing is the creational force. We create worlds within our minds, here we justify them, and reinforce them. We then manifest them in our lives with behavioral sets that rely upon our mental programming. These behaviors are dually reinforced in the social context, which we individually participate in. There is no world outside of our milieu and experience. If we travel outside of our milieu, that experience becomes a part of us as individuals, and is eventually fed into the social soup of which we individually exist in. There is no larger reality.

The world according to a man of color in a ghetto is similar yet disparate with respect to the young girl's world from Appalachia, North vs. South, Hawaiian vs. North Dakotan, etc. Nothing exists outside of this, their individual worlds. Nothing exists outside of this until a change occurs. Small changes create expansive social resonance such as Rosa Park's bus ride. Our belief makes it so. Our belief in a religion, or in a God breathes life into that God or Religion. Maybe we can't live without God. Certainly God cannot live without us, should man not have any record of a God. Should mankind entirely quell the rumbling of the religious, it is quite possible that God would become extinct.

As blasphemous as this train of thought seems, consider it from an anthropological perspective. How many cultures and belief systems have gone extinct on the face of the earth without our full knowledge of their doings? Their God became extinct. Consider the Easter Islanders, their religion and belief system is nearly inaccessible to us. Religion is a fun topic. I was very religious at one stage of my life, it truly helped me. To this day I remain very spiritual and believe that there is an infinite intelligence that is interested in harmony. Conversely, I think there must be a duality within the All that feeds off from chaos, entropy, and dissonance.

I believe that since you can lose everything, there truly is nothing.
I believe that nearly all of life's choices are crapshoots.

August 9, 2011

I am enjoying the sun and motorcycle ride. Motion and sunshine are two great gifts. I feel so alive embarking on this journey. We are traveling for fun and for a purpose. We are searching for clarity within the fabric of society. Clarity within our form of governance, clarity regarding poverty, class warfare, and our education system are all stops along the way. We are searching for particles of hope within American Democracy.

"Do not follow where the path may lead. Go instead where there is no path and leave a trail."

Ralph W. Emerson

Forever Yours,

Hermes Trismegistus (AKA Hermes)

Songs: *In The Ghetto,* Elvis Presley

Mother and Child Reunion, Paul Simon

LIBERTY

Mormonism & Me

I see myself, disembodied a 10 year old boy hiding in a chapel alcove. Still, quiet, waiting, safe from the troubles of home. The Church of Jesus Christ of Latter-Day Saints (Mormons) provided a safe harbor in my otherwise turbulent life. I would make phone calls on Saturday nights or Sunday mornings to arrange a car ride to church services. Later, as a young teen I would walk the eight or so miles each way to church. The congregation was always warm and inviting, close like how I imagined a family should be. The infants and children were never banished to a subterranean holding room, rather they were warmly welcomed and encouraged to give talks, and otherwise participate in the spiritual lessons.

The Mormon church has a rich albeit checkered history. Mormons believe in the King James Bible and Jesus. They believe in the strength found within families. They profess overall to live and let live, to not judge other people. Mormons believe that a faction of true believers departed from Jerusalem about 900 B.C. before it was sacked. Lehi, a righteous man, was called of God to be a prophet, to lead his family into the wilderness and eventually across the ocean to the Americas. Lehi's legacy was primarily carried on by one of his younger sons, Nephi. Nephi, a righteous man had trouble with his two older brothers; Laman and Lemuel. Mormonism posits that Nephi's descendants left a record of their spiritual happenings on golden plates, along with a post mortem visitation of Christ after his crucifixion. Hey, if Jesus could visit Mary and Esau, why not pre-Olmec ancestors...why not?

This spiritual legacy of ancient American prophets would not last. Wars and apostasy would decimate their spiritual culture. A sole survivor of ancient American prophets, Mormon alledgedly hid these gold and brass plates of record. In 1831 Joseph Smith, a fourteen year old boy of Palmyra, New York, prayerfully searched for his correct spiritual path and was allegedly visited by an angelic being that would later lead him to the ancient record hereto fore-mentioned. Mormons believe that Joseph was later baptized and ordained in the same priesthood from biblical times.

From there, the Mormon story sours for me. There are a few topics in Mormon history that are not talked about. I don't like the kind of cover-up secrets that some organizations vehemently brush under their rug and refuse to acknowledge…tell me the truth, the whole truth and nothing but the truth up front, don't let me stumble upon your secrets later, by myself. Joseph became a Freemason and later on created a temple system of initiations and ordinances. Uncannily, Joseph's ceremonies were identical to that of the Freemasons. In the Palmyra area was another Freemason, William Morgan. William had a falling out with the Freemasons and threatened to publish the Mason's rites, secret handshakes, etc. William came up missing, purportedly last seen being carted away by estranged Masonic friends. Joseph would later take William's widow as an extra wife. Joseph is said to have about twelve wives, much to the chagrin of his first wife.

Mormons are not aware of the fact that Joseph had other wives, nor are they aware that he was a Freemason, as were most of the early church leaders. When confronting the local lay-clergy of modern day Mormonism with the Masonic rites and Mormon temple similarities their response is usually, "They both probably came out of King Solomon's temple and traversed through history as two separate routes." This answer seems too uncanny, too suspect.

Later as the Mormons moved west, Joseph was killed by a mob. Brigham Young would take leadership of the church. An incident occurred called the Mountain Meadow Massacre. To their credit, the Mormons were on friendly terms with otherwise hostile Native Americans. A wagon train of non-Mormons was traveling through Mormon territory. Senior Mormon leaders made a tryst with the local Indians to attack the wagon train. Mormons dressed in native American attire and real natives formed a battle contingent. A five-day siege on the wagon train ensued. Allegedly, some Mormons agreed to broker a truce. The wagon train must put down their weapons. Men and boys march in front followed by women and girls. The Mormons and natives proceeded to attack the unarmed faction sparing only children under seven years old. Brigham would later deny any knowledge of this skirmish.

However, Mormon culture has always relied heavily upon top down leadership, loyalty to senior leadership, and communication to senior leadership. It is doubtful that within five days time word did not reach Brigham of this encounter. Brigham's participation in planning this skirmish before the five-day siege has always been suspect. Indeed it would be a mammoth and foolish leap of faith to believe that Brigham was not complicit in the Mountain Meadow Massacre. Most modern day Mormons have never heard of the Mountain Meadow Massacre, a convenient oversight.

I have met few Catholics that have knowledge of Jacques Demolay, the meaning of Friday the 13th, and the King Phillip-Pope Clement connection. Ignorance is an important ingredient in faith-based organizations, and Mormonism is no different.

Mormons have an organization headed by a modern day prophet. Yes a prophet, like Moses, Isaiah, and Joshua. The Prophet has a quorum of twelve apostles. Yes, apostles like Jesus' twelve apostles. The church is organized into stakes. Stakes are geographic regions like Dioceses. Within stakes are wards or branches. Branches are like wards just smaller. Each Ward has a lay clergy structure lead by a volunteer bishop. Reporting to the bishop is a group of high priests, sort of bishopric-emeritus. Also an elder's quorum president, which is another substructure of priesthood. The women's group is called relief society, they have a local volunteer president as well.

A young men's president leads the young men. The young men are considered priesthood holders of the Aaronic priesthood, a lower but still potent priesthood. The young men are subsequently separated into three subgroups, deacons, teachers, priests respectively by age. The young women are led by an adult young woman presidency and are further broken into three age-determined sub-factions. There is a local Sunday school presidency, again lay-volunteers that direct a small legion of volunteer teachers. The bishop oversees a small boon of other pet projects and volunteers: Family history volunteers, missionary committees, temple committees, building cleaning and maintenance volunteers, emergency preparedness focus groups, choirs, organists, and boy scouts to name a few.

Volunteer positions are filled through a mystical process of prayer by their to-be direct supervisors. In a perfect world a consensus is formed after one prayer and perusing the able and active name list. At the ward level the bishop and his counselor pray over the submitted name and approve or send the name back for re-prayer. Once a name is determined the bishop or his counselors call the dummy I mean candidate into their office and break the news to them. To refuse a calling is against church standards and mores', only very extenuating circumstances allow the schmuck…I mean candidate to opt out of the calling. Indeed, the candidate's standing and level of worthiness is based on upon their active participation in the church structure.

According to Gordon B. Hinckley, former prophet of the church, "Every worthy male should serve a "mission" (two year proselytizing). It doesn't take a doctoral degree in formal logic to understand the implications for the opposite of that statement. Implicit is if you are a young man of nineteen who doesn't serve a mission, you are not worthy…or substandard. The culture exudes this concept prolifically. From the time children are three or four years old they are singing "I hope they send me on a mission," coloring "I Want To Be a Missionary" activity sheets. Young woman are droned with the importance of supporting young men on missions, encouraging them to serve missions, and that it is by far preferential to marry a returned missionary (RM).

Boys at the age of nineteen are expected to fund and serve a mission for two years, wherever senior leadership in Utah "calls them to." That's right, missionaries don't choose their mission, God does through his appointed on earth, those riding around in a limo protected by LDS security services. Returned missionaries have joined a strong alumni.

This alumni within the church seems to wash each other's hands very well, advancing each other's careers, and church careers.

At the age of nineteen I dropped out of college to work and save for a mission. Traditionally, Mormon families help underwrite one's mission, as a young man works a few jobs and adds to their own mission fund kitty. Well if your family is not Mormon as mine was, you've got a problem. Usually senior members of the ward chip in and help out financially, becoming a surrogate family of sorts. For whatever reason, my ward members didn't. I cashiered at Kmart, bringing shopping carts in sleet and rain while simultaneously holding down two other jobs. I worked in a lumberyard tossing sixteen-foot boards as fast as a behemoth machine could toss them out. I served in a group home for the disabled, toileting, feeding, clothing, and nurturing them. My mom agreed to house me as long as I was working and saving for a mission. That arrangement lasted two months. In the bitter cold, February of 1996 she kicked me out, which as I was rarely there due to work. didn't seem to phase me at first.

Avoiding the added costs of rent and its accruements… I chose to sleep in my car in between these shifts. I let my bishop know of these developments. He was kinda of beside himself, unfamiliar with this surreal terrain. The language in the lumberyard break room was always unsavory, ergo I faithfully knelt in prayer amidst mountains of stacked lumber. Snow flitted in between the piles of ready to listen lumber. I poured my heart out, I begged, I cried, I thanked, I humbled, I prayed.

I slept often in the church parking lot, near the oversized dumpster. I had a battery powered clock set for a three-hour respite between jobs. Frost blanketed my windshield, snow peppered the dark night in between the orange glowing sidewalk light. Reclining in my car seat, a prayer of gratitude was on my lips as I dozed off. CRACK! CRACK!! CRACK!!! I startled awake to a penetrating light outside my car. The policeman asked me to unroll my window. "What are you doing here? Don't you have family you can live with? Your license and insurance card please. Wait right here." The officer disappeared into his heated cruiser for a heart-wrenching 20 minutes. No use in trying to sleep for the remaining 50 odd minutes.

About this time I knew deep down that I would not serve a mission. I would not be one of the worthy ones. That year would end in a combustion of futility and the death of a fallible yet real core strength in my life, my grandfather.

Mormons wear funny underwear. When Mormons go through the temple for the first time they participate in what's called an endowment. In the endowment Mormons take an oath to amongst other things, promise to wear sacred underwear that have markings of a Masonic nature on them. These mystical garments are purportedly rife with spiritual blessings and protection for those that wear them worthily.

Now, if you saw the garments, you would wonder how the dickens Mormons ever have large families. Mormon garments are pretty unsexy. Mormon garments include white knee-length knickers, and a high-necked t-shirt with regular sleeves, not the wife-beater variety. Mormons must wear the garments at all times, and cover the garments with regular clothing at all times. No mini-skirts, no shoulder strapped dresses. Somewhere there is a swimming clause though; you are allowed to wear normal swimwear without the garments. I think someone in Utah likes to splash around a bit.

Mormons are a close group of fellows; their schedules dictate intimacy. Sunday mornings consist at minimum of a three hour meeting schedule. That's right, three hours. One should weigh the options of going to a 40 minute Catholic Mass with their sit, stand, kneel, rise, call and answer routine, repeat, to the Mormon schedule of sitting for an hour, shuffling in between halls with quick quips of hello and guffaws, to be repeated again the next two hours.

If you have a "calling" you are usually early to church and late to leave while coordinating one project, lesson, or activity or another. Sometimes there are also evening meetings on Sunday. Mormons refrain from shopping, getting gas for their cars, swimming, sports, camping and most other forms of fun or productivity on Sundays. They don't drink coffee, caffeine, smoke, or believe in tattoos...they are all taboo! Twice a year there is a General Conference that is broadcast from the prophet and apostles in Utah. Rife with witty life lessons, reminiscing, and like *Chicken Soup for the Soul* anecdotes, the conference lasts all weekend with an hour or two break in between sessions. All members are highly encouraged to attend each session broadcast at their own meetinghouse.

Mondays are family home evening (FHE) nights. Families are encouraged to not plan any outside activity. FHE nights are family devotionals led by mom and dad including an opening prayer, family business (ie chore rosters, upcoming trips, concerns), a lesson (kids are encouraged to plan and provide lessons too!), church hymns, snack, board game or similar, and a closing prayer.

One night a week is a youth evening at church, sometimes combined meetings with girls and boys. Another night a week is for home-teaching. Home-teaching is a Mormon social work network. Men are paired by local church leadership and given a caseload of families to visit at least once a month. The average caseload is 5-6 families. I was once assigned a caseload of 18 families in college, at which point I didn't have a vehicle to visit anyone with. Hometeachers are to report the needs and status of their families to the elders' quorum leader who reports the same to the bishop. The system becomes kind of incestuous in small branches and wards. One person will be home taught by someone on their hometeaching list. Rumors spread easily within these cultures...gossiping...spiritual snobbery. So and so has a messy home, their child is or does...etc. The Relief Society (women's group) has the same system of hometeaching called visiting teaching, another layer of watchfulness, another form of information gathering and disseminating. On a good note, profound friendships usually do occur. Small miracles are manifested from financial need and welfare. A willingness to help one another out in halcyon days and nights of duress is forged. Humans are animals, and cliques will persist.

Friday night is considered date night. Married couples are encouraged to make time for an hour or so of personal adult time mono-a-mono. The relief society plans a homemaking night once a month, think Martha Stewart minus the Wall Street scandal. Mormon men are called to move fellow Mormons. Mormons tend to move a lot, and for whatever reason or origin, Mormon men are like well-trained movers. It's a workday of packing and loading up large families and their junk in caravans of domestic trucks, vans, and trailers. Someone always needs to be blessed and work parties are assigned or volunteered for such emergencies.

Mormons are strongly encouraged to start the day with personal prayer and scripture reading and finish the same way. Families are encouraged to add onto that daily prayer meetings. Mormons are strongly encouraged to research their family history, and to keep an active journal. Mormon time is filled to the brim and leaves little time for "outside influences." Outside influences is a term to identify anything in the community that would deprive one of the afore-mentioned schedule. Outside influences is a term to curb one's straying too far from the fold, a nice social control mechanism.

Mormons are required, not encouraged…required to tithe 10% of their gross income, not net income, and not what ever they feel inspired to tithe, 10% of their gross income is the commandment. One is "cursed with a curse" if they fail to tithe 10% of their gross income. Members meet annually with the bishop for tithing settlement to discuss their participation in the tithing program. The minimum standard of worthiness within the church depends upon one's fidelity to the tithing program. During the tithing settlement you make an oath to the bishop that you are tithing fully. Bishops have asked to see my pay stubs. During the tithing settlement the bishop probes you as to your participation in other permanent funds, such as a monthly fasting account, the missionary fund, building fund, and other pet projects.

The first Sunday of the month is Fast and Testimony meeting. No lessons or sermons are offered during the main Sunday service. It is open microphone day for congregates to relate lay-missionary experiences, how they "know the church is true," how they "know Joseph Smith was a real prophet of God and restored the *true* church." Children are encouraged to participate in this free-for all, the younger the better. It's usually a tearful moment for the testimony bearers. On Fast and Testimony days, all members including children are encouraged to refrain from food and liquids for 24 hours or a minimum of two meals. The rule of thumb is to donate the amount of money that they would have spent on food to the Fasting Fund. When I was a kid I was paired with an adult male to collect these Fasting Funds at the meetinghouse, and on a kind of car route. Those fasting and donating received extra spiritual blessings.

In the fall of 1996 I applied to college again, Plattsburgh State University. The first day I was there was a Sunday. I went to the Mormon church and met my wife-to-be, a charming story on it's own. Mormons get married in the temple, not death do us part but for all time and eternity. Children born to temple-married parents are born in the covenant and are automatically sealed to their parents, again for all time and eternity.

In order to be married in the temple, couples must go through a series of interviews with the bishop and stake president. Mormons believe in being chaste before marriage, no cheating! Our stake president lived across Lake Champlain, an hour by ferry and about another hour's drive. Stake presidents are usually top-level executives in the real world. Getting an appointment with a stake president is usually a 2-3 month process and a miracle in its own right. We had planned on getting married in the Washington D.C. temple, that beautiful structure that seems to rise out of the earth on the 495 beltway, can't miss it...looks like you'll drive right into it!

Having unstable in-laws is not fun. The stake president handed our temple recommends (a paper license that has a UPC code of sorts) to Steph my bride. Steph lived at home. Steph's mom, a Mormon in relatively good standing... stole our recommends hoping to block our nuptials. With less than a week to go before our departure to the D.C.

temple we scrambled to get a second copy made up from the bishop, then the stake president. We essentially had to elope. We returned as husband and wife, and it was an uncomfortable scene on Sundays with the mother in-law fuming over our marital maneuver.

One Sunday, just as the women and men had separated for our respective meetings, as I bowed my head in group prayer within the chapel my mother in-law slammed opened the chapel doors "take his fucking priesthood away!!! He is a no good lying motherfucker!!!…" This went on for sometime, and the next thing I remember I was in the bishop's office. It was a very cold year in Plattsburgh. There was an ice storm and the national guard was called in to help restore roads, electricity etc. I had lost my driver's license from speeding tickets and falling asleep at the wheel the year before, going in between those jobs with no sleep! Stephanie's parents had refused to let her get her driver's license, it would have given her more independence, she was 22 years old.

I taught Stephanie how to drive, so she could get her license and we wouldn't have to walk everywhere in the cold. Did we go on long fun road trips? No. I taught her how to parallel park, how to make turns, how to switch lanes, all of this done on abandoned streets and dirt roads. The mother in-law found out about it. That's what her tirade was about that Sunday. The bishop wanted to know if it was true, was I teaching Stephanie how to drive. Up to this point, I had always done whatever the leadership had asked; it's the culture. Being naïve and a purist at the time, I told him yes. The bishop confiscated my temple recommend and put me on a form of probation. I became a pariah within the congregation for some time. Probation in the Mormon church is a horrendous place to be. Your priesthood is suspended, you are emasculated…You cannot say a prayer in church. Indeed, you do not have a prayer until the bishop, of his own whim, decides to reinstate you.

There is no due process, or form of appeals. The bishop's decision is final, and it's added to your church record in Utah. Wherever you go, your church record will follow you. Lord have mercy on your soul if your home or visiting teachers find something to report to the bishopric!

One of my dearest friends, a sweet gentle, kind loving Christian and fellow Mormon was put on probation for over six years without any specific accusation lodged against him… He is just quirky, creative, and eccentric.

Mormon woman must wear dresses on Sundays, not dress pants, or business suits. Men should wear white shirts and ties, no beards or mustaches. There must be a church approved medical reason for men to have facial hair. Mormon culture is all consuming.

Religion is the problem. Spirituality is a personal relationship with the Divine. Religion is dogma, organizational structure, volunteership, buildings, checking accounts, a set of behaviors that inculcate heritage. Religion is often at odds with spirituality. I would like to imagine no religion. I find that the greatest indictment to be leveled against the Mormon church is the fact that they are just like any other religion. Namely they are interested in money, membership, and manpower, can you imagine any religion without them?

I think that it is entirely possible that there were ancient Hebrews that traveled to the Americas. Ever read Kon Tiki by Thor Heyerdal? It's even possible that Joseph Smith received an angelic vision, ever hear of the Lady of Lourdes or Fatima? All of that could be true and yet everything could be still wrong. My own spiritual journey has found an often-overlooked theme from most forms of scriptures. Judaic, Moslem or other Eastern prophets and visionaries were fallible yet were still entrusted with Divine awareness and messages.

When weighing the pros and cons of religious observance, and the importance of religious experience in my life, I have concluded that religion should point one to the Divine. One should then matriculate to a rich personal experience with the divine that surpasses and transcends the divisiveness of dogma; religion. Still, for comfort, for those lost, for those that desire to help others that are lost, religion can be a great experience to forward the Divine's message. Gandhi encouraged Catholics to remain Catholic, Jews to remain Jewish, etc. because that would be the means or symbolic language by which the Divine would communicate to them; an interesting concept. So I take my boys to the Mormon church…sparingly…very sparingly.

I believe that belief is a creative force, see the Maharishi Effect.

I believe that there is a lot more to fear than fear itself!

LIBERTY

Lincoln, Liberty And Love

We pose for a few pictures on the wide slide. Back to camp to cook hotdogs and s'mores over the fire with sticks. The boys love doing this. Everyone is exhausted and heads to bed with kid camp food filled bellies. Hermes and I both start a vigil. Hermes stands nobly on the picnic table next to the citronella can candle throwing orange light into the inky night. Hermes and I both note that there is a Hassidic Jew family camped next us. A Jew proceeds with his own tireless vigil of pacing back and forth, making a rhythmatic bow at each end of his path.

Trains, planes and automobiles fill up the space of the night reminding us that our forest is smack-dab in the middle of a large metropolis. Hermes and I both note that our camp neighbors have read the writing on my clothing, but do they know its meaning? Some questions are irrelevant. I have penned in Hebrew an apocryphal statement from Revelations. This added notion might be shtick, it might be part of my insanity, it might be a valid proposition, or it might be a combination of all of these elements. Time will tell, and in time I will tell what I wrote.

Which is more important peace and subjectivity or the kind of violence that creates, consumes, and conquers? Hermes asks with a booming voice of which I am fearful the family will wake up to. In my life, which is all I can answer to peace and subjectivity are the only choice. I have no other choice. I am a eunich. Besides Hermes, isn't there another choice somewhere? Why must you be either or all the time?! I fire back to him with furrowed brow. Can't violence camouflage for peace and peace for violence? I counter without allowing him an iota of time to wedge dissonance between my ears. Silence.

Hermes, all of these things…violence, peace, anger, love are states of mind that originate within a person. I added this in a calm subdued tone. True we can control very little external factors in our life, who, when, where we were born to. Much of our past is immutable, and our past has made us. Yet somewhere within us, somehow we can consciously make a choice; A new direction. A better way of life. This choice is called grace. Grace is the indomitable spirit to not only take things with a grain of salt, to not just accept the past and all the bad or wrong in life, but to rise above it. Grace is the conscious conviction to not be sullied or dissuaded from your personal happiness in the long run. You may be temporarily perturbed, frustrated, full of rage, and even make foolish mistakes, wrong turns. Grace demands that we rise above the turmoil and find the beauty within ourselves, your own genius that sometimes whispers and oft times screams "I am good, and will overcome".

LIBERTY

August 9, 2011

Dear Joe and Rosa,

Yesterday was a big hot day! I went to the nation's capital! The White House, WWII Memorial, The George Washington Memorial, and the Abraham Lincoln Memorial. Everywhere we went, there were Secret Service officers. A black motorcade pulled up to the White House and a sniper was stationed on the roof!

There certaintly is a lot of hustle and bustle out there… in the big world! Not sure if I am losing myself or finding myself… But it will all work out in the end!

All My Love,

Hermes

Songs: *Let it Be,* Beatles

End of the Line, Traveling Wilbury's

Click, the stereo turns on *"Light one candle for the pain they endured when their right to exist was denied."* Click-click static click, *"We are bound together by the task that stands before us, and the road that lies ahead... we are bound...shed a little light."* The music faded like tired grandpa exhaling in his sleep.

I lit a candle. I realize that my journey is just beginning. It was a restless night for me. The crickets were angry, their feverish leg rubbing sounded uncomfortable for them and me. Stars dotted the night and glittered through the dancing trees. The tarp that I laid on made crumpling sounds. My shirt for a pillow, I tossed and turned between the angst of life and what is; between a rock and a hard place.

Morning came as it always does. A quick breakfast of juice and pastry, we broke camp and took turns at punctuated visits to the restroom. Steph again clambered on top of the car, stuffing the car top carrier in her own indecipherable way. A quick and impromptu meeting rehashing the day's itinerary then we headed out for the day. I thought that we needed 695. It would take us to 495. We must have missed it, and we ended up at a busy port. I burned my leg a few times on the muffler. Swearing only helps the ego in these cases. I swore. After a 45-minute detour we turned around and got on 495. The plan was to enter Washington D.C. from the west. From west of D.C. we would park and take the subway in. We finally found a parking lot nearly full around Vienna. Not sure motorcycles can park here…I'm the only one. We park, I put sunscreen on the boys and myself.

Talk about a cultural experience! After taking a subway every day for years, travel to the country. After living in the country for decades, take a subway in. Different modalities of transportation, different perspectives on life, on how to interact or not interact, different stops on the life train. I'm sure we stuck out like sore thumbs, country rubes in the metropolis. The boys made fast and friendly acquaintances. Funny how a child's smile can melt most hearts and tear down walls.

Mankind's quest for liberty begins after, and only after, his basic needs are met. Man has no other higher purpose than to fill his belly, have warm comfortable shelter, and basic securities in life. The one and only exception to this rule arises when mankind is oppressed and tyrannized by another man who hoards the basic resources of life.

Ipso facto, in the last scenario, freedom from such a tyrannical rule gnaws at the denizens' gut, mind, and soul. History has shown that the many are caught up in an unrelenting dance with the few in order to secure a modicum of liberties and a week's worth of food. This is democracy; two wolves and a sheep voting over what to eat for lunch. B. Franklin

The purpose of the few is to always manipulate the many. To manipulate the populaces' resources. To manipulate the human resource, the capital, and especially the level of contentment felt by the satus quo. When the many have two cars, a home, and a vacation once a year, things are good and no one need think of the poor or extreme elite. When the times dry up, and many people lose their homes, propaganda fills the airwaves. Propaganda that insists things will get better. The many cannot share the plight of the poorest for too long or revolution will be afoot.

Few people have ever fought the good fight. The good fight demands that caste systems cease and desist. Liberty has missed its mark. Liberty has only risen to a half-baked notion in America and throughout history for that matter. President Franklin Delano Roosevelt (FDR) understood the schism that separates the poor from real citizens of liberty. FDR argued "We have come to a clear realization of the fact that true individual freedom cannot exist without economic security and independence. "Necessitous men are not free men. People who are hungry and out of a job are the stuff of which dictatorships are made."

Individual economic security and rights are directly tied to a nation's overall freedom and form of leadership whether it be a humane and true democracy or a tyrannical plutocracy.

A second Bill of Rights was forwarded by one of America's best presidents. FDR developed an Economic Bill of Rights that has never been enacted in America. The second bill of rights has laid dormant at liberty's feet waiting for humanity to lift this torch, wield it against its antagonists, and light the way for all peoples. President Roosevelt proposed the following bill of rights for all Americans regardless of race or creed:

The right to a useful and remunerative job in the industries or shops or farms or mines of the nation;

The right to earn enough to provide adequate food and clothing and recreation;

The right of every farmer to raise and sell his products at a return, which will give him and his family a decent living;

The right of every businessman, large and small, to trade in an atmosphere of freedom from unfair competition and domination by monopolies at home or abroad;

The right of every family to a decent home;

The right to adequate medical care and the opportunity to achieve and enjoy good health;

The right to adequate protection from the economic fears of old age, sickness, accident, and unemployment;

The right to a good education.

"All of these rights spell security. And after this war is won we must be prepared to move forward, in the implementation of these rights, to new goals of human happiness and well being. America's own rightful place in the world depends in large part upon how fully these and similar rights have been carried into practice for all our citizens. For unless there is security here at home there cannot be lasting peace in the world." FDR

William, my oldest son, has become enamored with President Lincoln and enchanted with the Civil War. During this journey we will show him Abraham Lincoln and teach him about the man, his times, his talent, and his challenges. We're headed for the nation's capitol. We're on a mission. We go to the National Mall and arrive above ground like country moles. The Washington Monument pierces the sky, a phallic symbol from ancient Egypt. The heat withers our strength as we pass the White House on the right. The Lincoln Memorial straight ahead, we turn heels and stomp our way through the oppressive heat towards the effigy of America's liberator.

The World War II monument has been installed since my last sojourn here. William is aware that he was named after my grandfather, a World War II vet. William speaks in his kind yet choppy language, "Your granddad William's war?" Will speaks in a wonderful singsong; he's a bright boy with some difficulty in speech. William is marvelously creative, analytical, perceptive, kind, generous, and well behaved. His brother and he are the apples of my eyes. I don't know how much they will remember of this trip, but I planned it all for them. I want to inculcate them in the principles of peace, of government, of shared heritage, of our nation's mistakes and glowing moments…and I must do this when they are young!

The World War II memorial lies at the feet of the elongated rectangle pool found on the national mall. Water falls into the war memorial from the direction of the rectangle pool. The war memorial hallows out space in an amphitheatre format. Famous quotes line the walls, benches surround the reflection pool, wreathes of peace are upheld by eagles, within covered domes at the cardinal direction points. A moment of sacredness overcomes us. We bask in the bravery of these national heroes and heroines. Time finds us at the opposite end of the memorial, and swiftly upon the torn up reflection pool. Men and machines dot the bare soil where support pile-ons protrude haphazardly. We follow this surreal scene along a shaded avenue. Our drinking water seems to evaporate between our mouths and the bottle top. Grandpa treats the boys to ice cream bars dished out from street vendors. We share a concrete street lamp base, a reprieve for our tired toes.

The Lincoln Memorial rises like a temple out of the ground. The boys glare up at the flights of stairs. Daddy carry me please? Sweat drips off every corner of my body, a blister is forming on my footpad. Sure boys, Haydn first because he asked first, then you Will. I am the family sherpa toting the snacks, drinks, camera, maps, and sunscreen etc. Hermes also demanded that I heft him to each site, bossy gnome that he is!

No one knows Abraham Lincoln, least of all Lincoln himself. Lincoln was depressed, suicidal, at one time anti-Christian and a fatalist. A fatalist believes that nothing can be done to change what is or will be. Some argue that Lincoln had intimate relationships with men. At one point Lincoln was very much into mysticism, spiritualism and séances. Very few people liked him; even his closest cabinet members had less than favorable views on him. On the day that he was to deliver the Gettysburg Address, Lincoln had to wait as a local pundit delivered an oration over two and a half hours. Tersely, Lincoln was instructed that day to "Keep it short Mr. President," as few people cared to hear what Lincoln had to say. Lincoln composed an epistle of less than 300 words, which would insure his immortality upon humanity. Few people have articulated the immutable laws of humanity so succinctly and inspirationally before or after him.

Lincoln lost many political races, and was a failed businessman. He at one time believed that African Americans should be sent back to

LIBERTY

Africa, or to an island somewhere. Lincoln did believe that slavery was repugnant. Politically, he foresaw the death of slavery slowly, by not letting slavery spread to the west. Lincoln did not emancipate the slaves in the beginning of the Civil War. Emancipating slaves in the beginning of the war would have ignited an already robust anti-Lincoln faction in the North, and pro-slavery sympathizers of the west and north. Lincoln delivered the Emancipation Proclamation only as the South was on its last leg; a coup de grace. It could be argued that Lincoln's emancipation of the slaves was a political and martial act more than a humanitarian watershed moment. All of this begs the question: who is this megalithic man that sits enshrouded in mystery before me, cool and composed during the blazing August heat?

Lincoln's memory has entered the status of ancient and august legend, like tales of ancient pharaohs. Do we know who this man was? Can scholars and academicians come to a consensus and shed light on the life of Lincoln? How will we teach our children who Lincoln was, what he stood for, and about his shortcomings? Turning inward I ask who am I? Who is the clerk in my hometown grocery? Our perceptions and sustaining belief systems create and destroy a person or persons. I am no Lincoln scholar. I know Abraham Lincoln to be passionate, intemperate personally and sagaciously tempered politically. Lincoln haunts me. His words tug at my throat, I am bound by his masterful notions: *to create a MORE perfect union...*

I truly wonder if we are more free now, given where we are now as a country with minority rights, equality, and obtaining the wanderlust vision of yore, namely to be free, to attain a level of happiness and equality, to disrobe the archaic and oppressive systems of days gone past. Have the institutions of slavery, fiefdom, indentured servitude or caste systems resurfaced in our fine country under another name? The Lincoln memorial is crowded. Hermes draws a lot of nice yet awkward attention; it's time to bounce. The blister on my foot causes me to limp all the way to the White House. I carry the boys intermittently, our day pack constantly, and the questions and notions that swirl in my head only add to the heat and pressure of the day.

Photos in front of the White House, Secret Service layered upon layers. A black motorcade arrives at the White House, sniper stands guard…not much to see here. Not sure how effectual and powerful the position of president is these days anyways. Time to go. We seek food and shelter from the heat in a subterranean way-place before boarding the subway for points west, away from the nagging questions, away from the world of politics and faux promises. Stephanie decides that she urgently needs to toilet after we arrive at our car and Spirit. Liberty always waits, always lurks vigilantly, Liberty is an afterthought to necessity. Fear keeps Liberty in check. Fear devours liberty.

I believe that sometimes one should dig their heals in and fight

And other times one should roll over and play dead.

LIBERTY

August 11, 2011

Dear Joe and Rosa,

I am enjoying the Nation's Capital! It's great being a tourist. I don't intend to sound ungrateful. However it feels like I am a foreigner visiting my own federal sites. I mean do these people really represent me? Are their life experiences and agendas similar or in sync with mine?

The first country in the world to declare "for the people by the people" has not lived up to its own hype. Return the power to the people now!

Go home if you are not a gnome!

Forever Yours,

Hermes Trismegistus (AKA Hermes)

Songs: *Fortunate Son,* Credence Clearwater Revival

Jackson, Johnny Cash and June Carter

MH Kisner

Case Study In American Education And Democracy

The cool breeze is refreshing and life giving. No more will I dwell on the weighty things we encountered today, at least for now. We are clipping at a good pace on route 66 west, a route I know all too well. Steph and I taught at-risk kids outside D.C. We could not afford to live near our work, so we commuted an hour and a half each way, everyday. We still paid $1100 a month for rent, no utilities, not furnished etc. Such is the state of America. Most teachers cannot afford to live near their schools. Teachers are supposed to have a cakewalk, a fluff job. After all they get so much time off, summers, winter, spring breaks and federal holidays. What no one tells you is that most teachers work 12 hours a day when in session.

Teachers must develop written lesson plans, school assignment sheets for students, grade papers, and call-write-and meet with parents. Teachers usually belong to two or three subcommittees that meet after school, not to mention district wide required training, mandatory licensing testing, and requalification through more and more college classes. During summer break, school administrators are taking note of teachers that are actively working within their classrooms throughout the summer. Absentee teachers usually don't fare well with administrators. The week immediately following school summer break, teachers must inventory, pack, remove or stowaway nearly all of the school supplies in their room, much of which they purchased from their own nominal wage. The week before school is an all-hands-on-deck flurry of meetings, training, unpacking and setting up one's classroom. Teaching is anything but a cakewalk.

More and more, teachers are held accountable for factors infinitely beyond their control. Class sizes are ballooning, resources are shrink-

LIBERTY

ing, and wages are nowhere in the ballpark for the lifestyle and requisite education level to become a teacher. If Johnny has behavioral problems, it is not Johnny's fault, its not his parents responsibility to curb or help him; Johnny's behavior is not within the administrator's purview. Johnny's behavioral issues are the teacher's problem fin'. Of which, a school administrator can stack the deck, curry favor, or decimate a teacher's career by putting six Johnny's in one class to scuttle a teacher's career, and boost another's. Administrators can yield a sword of career destruction by belittling a teacher's perceived classroom management, lesson plans, or teaching savvy. There is no recourse for a teacher. Teacher unions? Pshaw! Most are too chummy with administrators to maintain an iota of unbiased credence. To be a teacher is to be insane.

Sitting in the principal's office yet again. This time I am an adult. This time the school principal is the one in trouble, she just doesn't know it yet. I was there visiting the school to observe my son in his class. It was a cordial meeting albeit riddled with lies and deceit on her part.

The principal was objecting to classroom observations. She persuaded me to believe that ultimately it was her prerogative as to who or whether or not parents could visit their child's classroom. According to this principal, having parents observe their child would violate the privacy of other students, and would be disruptive to the classroom routine. A salvo of letter writing ensued. The superintendent chose solidarity with the principal's position. I contacted Albany, the Department of Education. About this time I started to research the provenance of the principal's claims. All of her positions were erroneous and illegally founded. Which is scarier: A). the principal is unawares of basic school law or B). The principal is aware of widely publicized and basic education law and persists in lying to you and breaking that law?

Initially, the contact in Albany chose to stand behind the principals' position *even* after I pointed out the legislation found within Title 1, NCLB, and state education law! The following fact is the only thing that would turn the tide and allow justice to prevail. I contacted the Attorn

General, who in turn referred me to the State Comptroller. I presented the facts to the State Comptroller via an email and carbon copied it to all concerned. The State Comptroller agreed with my point and voiced over a phone conversation what everyone on the streets had been asking "what are they trying to hide?"

Within four weeks, I received an email from the school superintendent inviting me to observe my son in the upcoming school session. My final words to all parties encouraged more cooperation at the district level, more oversight at the state level, and a cautionary message relating that very few parents in this rural area would have the know-how and self-esteem to follow this path to attain the liberties already afforded them through legislation.

THE AMERICAN EDUCATION SYSTEM:
Points to Improve Upon

Not everything that can be counted counts and

not everything that counts can be counted.

Albert Einstein.

Award winning educator and author John Taylor Gatto has a unique view on the education system past and present. Gatto argues that schools often invoke an archaic set of laws wielded by kings, parens patriae. Gatto reminds us that schools act as parents during the day and usually have the full legal right to act in the parental role. At one time kings had such rule over their citizens.

Having such ultimate authority and kingly discretion can be a bad thing. Our education has and continues to operate on flawed reasoning. Gatto purports that in his 30 plus year tenure as an award winning teacher he has never truly met a gifted and talented student and has very rarely met a learning disabled student. Rather, these are just labels and mechanisms that suit the adult education community more than they serve the child's needs.

One's faith in standardized testing should be rocked to its core as Gatto points out that most school superintendents have the lowest score on the Graduate Record Exam in comparison with people of equal education levels in other fields. Is the test valid and reliable at measuring intellectual ability or are many superintendents intellectual bottom feeders? How can superintendents be the greatest champions for testing achievement within their school districts if their own standardized testing is lackluster?

Gatto illuminates small and large policies that fail the children and the communities of especially urban school environs. The author argues that bureaucracy of large layers of systems upon systems is one major area of failure within education. Indeed the education system has become a lumbering Frankenstein wreaking more and more havoc (p. xxxiii). As all bureaucracies are shouldered by the many silent participants Gatto forwards the notion that indifference is a system imperative, it would collapse from its contradictions if too much sensitivity entered the operating system (p.80). Education must be dehumanized to maintain its bureaucratic form. Person to person stuff is contrary to policy. *That's why popular teachers are disliked and fired* (italics added). They *talk* to kids. It's unacceptable (p. 204).

Gatto further relates what I discovered all too painfully and personally. The micro politics of schooling is degrading, disgusting, and demoralizing…(p. 340). The exigencies of day-to-day schooling can be difficult to fathom. Moral codes don't drive school decision-making. That means schools sometimes decides to ignore the wimpy kid being beaten up for lunch money in order to oil some greater wheels. School has no tear ducts with which to weep (p. 305).

A school administrator's job isn't about children: it's about systems maintenance (p. 306). Gatto continues to outline our current education system and it's development from it's conception to its current state of affairs. The author paints a real dystopian nightmare within our current education system. In fact, it is only through small flashes in the pan of his tome that we are made to understand what real education could look like. Gatto boils the problem down to this: H*ere is the crux of the difference between education and schooling – the former turns on independence, knowledge, ability, comprehension, and integrity, the latter upon obedience* (p. 153).

Gatto's assessment and prognosis of our current public school system is bleak. He relates, no public school in the United States is set up to allow a George Washington to happen. Washingtons in the bud stage are screened, browbeaten, or bribed to conform to a narrow outlook on social truth (p. 153). And, schools train individuals to respond as a mass (p. 42). I certainly found these axioms enforce within my schooling experience including my graduate studies.

Gatto's prophetic message that the fallout of a failed economy, plus a failed education system, plus an underemployed-schooled generation portends a need and subsequent rise in police and policing. Many people like Gatto see the writing on the wall. Gatto's stance focuses on the education systems' failure as a catalyst for America going the way of Rome. I don't agree with every idea or sentence that Gatto forwards. However, he presents a cogent and thorough intellectual and socio-political pedigree that fingers our education policies and practices as a mechanism to oppress the poor and manufacture a complacent, illiterate, and apathetic labor force sans learning, sans education, sans liberty.

Author Diane Ravitch illuminates some of the problems within the American education system. Ravitch argues that standardized tests are not precise instruments. Yet many educators and policymakers act as if standardized tests are accurate. Ravitch states that student performance may be affected by the weather, the student's state of mind, distractions outside the classroom, or conditions inside a classroom. *Tests may also become invalid if too much time is spent preparing students to take them* (p. 153, italics added). Many teachers solely teach to the test, as their career depends upon a favorable outcome of their wards. Yet Ravitch states that No Child Left Behind (NCLB) produces mountains of data, not educated citizens (p. 29).

According to Ravitch, students often have a lower motivation for learning and an erosion of science and math skills due to an over testing emphasis created by NCLB (p. 29). An egregious method of improving your odds as a teacher to obtain high scores from your students is to find ways to exclude poor testers from the testing pools. There are outsourced sub-groups, which won't directly affect a classes scores on NCLB testing. The more a teacher can sort and outsource low performing students from her testing pool, the higher her classes score soars. This is beneficial for her career status and advancement.

English as a second language, special education students and other sub-groups of students can be sorted out of her main testing pool. Ipso facto, the more a low scoring child is labeled and sorted out for real or imagined services, the easier it is to manage a class and obtain that all important NCLB test score. At what cost does this sub-group labeling occur? How much time can a student spend outside of a classroom being socialized differently than his cohorts and still have a learning self-esteem intact and gain a comparable education?

Ravitch highlights the fact that students are drilled and prepared for NCLB tests months before the actual test date which ignores the students' interests while promoting the interests of adults who take credit for non-existent improvements (p. 159).

The author defines her own belief that a democratic nation cannot sustain itself if its citizens are uninformed and indifferent about its history, its government, and the workings of its economy (p.223). Learning and literacy across the fields of government, economics, and history are integral to sustaining democracy. When we fail within our education system, we fail as a nation.

Ravitch contends that if we don't treasure our individualists, we will lose the spirit of innovation, inquiry, imagination, and dissent that has contributed powerfully to the success of our society… (p. 226). Are we teaching complacency or are we teaching our youth the powerful skills of rebellion so righteously required to maintain a true democracy?

John Merrow adds his voice to the discussion of American education. He professes *I think it's time to be impatient, to be mad as hell and not willing to take it anymore* (p. xix, italics added). This is the spirit of revolution of ownership of the problems and solutions that face the education system. Strong measures are needed to save public education (p. 10). Merrow's voice echoes Gatto's in that ...*giving children maximum opportunities to learn and grow is rarely anyone's highest priority* (p. 21). Liberty and education are duly connected from Merrow's perspective; without an effective and efficient system of public education, our democracy will wither and die (p. 69).

How can we make a more pure union within our education system? Merrow succinctly identifies four areas for improvement: Opportunity, expectations, affection, and outcomes. Merrow argues that these four domains need an overhaul within our education system. What will become of our nation if we don't have a revolution even just within our education system let alone our domestic and foreign policies? How low can we go in global education standing, and still be a leader in the free world? Have we already passed the Rubicon of timeframe to be able to do anything lasting and effective within our education system? What shall our progeny inherit by way of educational strengths and weaknesses say fifty years from now.

I believe its never fun fighting the inevitable.

I believe that "life is what happens to you

while you're busy making other plans." John Lennon

LIBERTY

Pushing Boundaries In Law Enforcement & Quantum Physics

We merge onto 81 South. Our pace quickens, we exit on 264. The Blue Ridge Mountains tower above us to the left. In life we must go through hills and valleys. We are all faced with a dark night of the soul at one point or another in life. I must travel to where I died, I must face the demons that will forever eat at my soul. Everyone has a threshold, a breaking point. Many people are never faced with it.

Luray is a cozy neighborhood at the eastern foot of a mountain path. We pull into our hotel parking lot across from the Sheriff's department. I reckon this is one of the most dangerous locations in the county. Officer Brown Shirt of Page County fame was indicted on 22 felonious counts. Officer Brown Shirt was involved in embezzlement, participating in cockfighting, sexual *assault* (not harassment) in the workplace, the list went on and on. Maybe Officer Brown Shirt doesn't exemplify all of the noble women and men that don the blue or brown uniform. Who polices the police is the question. The FBI got involved in this case, after over ten years of who-knows what level of abuse and corruption. I've followed state troopers that have broken half a dozen traffic laws within four miles. Who will write these troopers a ticket? If I call the barracks and report them, the first question that is asked is *what is your name and where do you live?* Not a comfortable line of questioning for any joe-citizen to answer. I've never heard of any follow-up from such a reporting. I've never seen an officer in traffic court reporting to a judge as to why they broke traffic laws in their cruiser without an emergency related excuse, it won't happen in our society.

Listen carefully here. *Every nation or dynasty's demise was in large part due to an untamed police force,* without exception. Martial law is possible in America and has been considered in recent years due to financial failure of our economy. As spurious as it sounds, even ascertaining martial law portends the failure of democracy, study well world history.

The numbers never add up for the American peasant, the lion's share of our populace. I have attended traffic court where more than a dozen citizens were being fined for inadequate mufflers. I will call the traffic lawbreakers idiots, not to belittle them rather, to identify their existence. The idiots were being fined, and brought before a judge. Their initial encounter was with a police officer on the street. In the courtroom, the idiots were greeted by a prosecutor; a hired lawyer. The lawyer invariably gave them all a wonderful deal; about $40 and one point discount if they accepted the bargain. As the prosecutor wryly added, "this is a great deal, if you go before the judge you probably won't get this break." One by one, the idiots lined up like ducks to accept the offer.

Each idiot added to the county coffer. Not one idiot questioned authority, the process, the rationale, and due process to circumvent themselves from their pricey predicament. When will we stop oppressing the poor!? On another day, a town officer alleged that I traveled across the yellow line illegally. I showed up to the pre-trial hearing and refused to take the "bargain," against the advice of the judge that reminded me that this would be the best offer that I would receive, and that it would be just the judge, myself and the prosecutor involved should we go to trial. I retorted that this was sloppy police work from beginning to end, the officer didn't even type in my name correctly, I am innocent, and I demand a trial as is my legal right.

What the afore-mentioned idiots don't realize is: It is very costly for the officer and judge to have a hearing. A stenographer must be present, the officer is usually required to be there (not available to bring in revenue for that day), the prosecutor must develop and prepare a case *beyond a reasonable doubt,* and a cadre of clerks must send notices, file away papers etc. Not to mention that the officer, judge, and prosecutor have their careers in broad daylight and somewhat online during a real trial that these spoofs at the democratic process called pre-trial (bargain) hearings.

LIBERTY

Guess what happened to me for my trial? After hours of preparation, research, dressing in a suit, arranging time off from work, and a babysitter for two days (the pre-trial and trial dates), the officer failed to attend. He was a no-show. How rude, unprofessional and disrespectful!!! I won my case by default. I didn't pay a fine, my insurance didn't hike, and no points were added to my record, all of which were successes compared to what I was offered at the pretrial. Was it a victory for democracy? Not by a long shot.

I lost the two days of work pay, babysitter, and travel. The prosecutor, judge, and officer's reputation and batting average were left intact. I think I should be entitled to the remuneration of my costs, including the amount of the fine/surcharge of the ticket. What is this if it is not harassment? Why did the officer fail to call and cancel ahead of time? What would happen if I failed to call ahead and cancel? Why are those rules different for the officer than the citizen?

Back in the hotel, safe in the shadow of the sheriff's office(?). The air conditioner is throwing sweet nectar at my sun burnt and dehydrated body. Tom and I head down to the pool with the boys. Trying not to think of anything, I am forced to experience things deeply. I try to shake off specters of yesteryear…Abe Lincoln…begone, Danny Pesgraves…

tah-tah, legions of uniformed goons going after idiots… fall away! After all of this conscious banishment, I am left with even more demonic poltergeists that have their way with my internal programming.

The boys are full of energy as they have been safely restrained in the back seat for hours of travel. Grandpa is quite a sight in his cutoffs held up by suspenders and untied work boots. *Hey grandpa! No sweaters in the pool!!* We have a delicious banter. We flop and swim by ourselves for close to two hours. Hunger sits in and gnaws at our bellies. We head upstairs and rally the troops for dinner at McDonalds.

We order twice the amount of food we normally eat. Haydn eats too quickly and gets sick in the lobby, then the bathroom. I'm embarrassed and feel bad for my little man. He's fine, he adds. I make phone calls to dear friends when we get back to the hotel. I've made arrangements to meet my Reiki (ray key) pals.

Reiki is an alternative form of healing. I was the furthest away from this mystical path for the first 33 years of my life. Just as a dog whistle's intonation is beyond our normal level of perception, just as $E=MC^2$ means that all things are vibrating, our bodies, and their components vibrate. Reiki is an ancient form of manipulating the body's energy to generate better health.

Reiki has three levels or degrees. Level one is an introductory course where students learn basic meditation and breathing exercises. Many level one students develop "Reiki hands," a warm tingling sensation in one's hands while giving Reiki or being in close proximity to another that needs Reiki.

Reiki two students learn three symbols that assist healing. Reiki two students begin to practice distance healing, sending energy across time and space just as you would pray for a loved one far away. Reiki two students generally have "shake-ups" in their lives whereas people and circumstances can change drastically in their lives in order to lose the dross, or incorrect paths from their lives. Reiki three is the master level. Reiki masters gain two more symbols. They can teach and attune other people from Reiki one to three. More shake-ups can be expected at this level. Inevitably, you will end up teaching and attuning even if you chose Reiki three for only personal development. Reiki masters are shown their many faults and areas for improvement. Spiritual development occurs within individuals first.

I have experienced irrefutable and profound things whilst giving or receiving Reiki. In John Denver's autobiography, he is very open regarding his infertility and hope to be a biological father. For many years he tried to father a child naturally. John went through a Reiki session and two weeks later they were with child. It's doubtful that this was a chance correlation. We know so little. Edgar Cayce was a devout Christian from the bible belt, uneducated. Edgar Cayce was able to identify and prescribe treatments for sick people thousands of miles away with profound accuracy and recovery rates. Cayce told us that we could all attain this skill if we but practice and work on it through meditation, prayer etc. I tend to believe that spirituality and science converge at the quantum level.

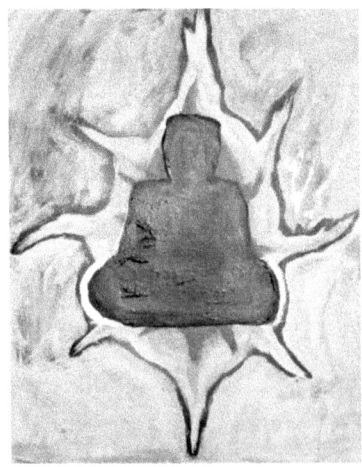

In my own neophyte studies I find that there is a malleable energy field where thought can guide and direct some outcomes on the physical plane. We are only touching the surface of quantum understanding but what we do know, these small yet dynamic puzzle pieces create a fantastic panorama. The Maharishi Effect occurs when one percent of a population meditates, prays, or otherwise consciously expects an improvement in a social problem. One percent of a school population can reduce violence just by focusing on improvement.

Cymatics is another mind-boggling science. Cymatics is the study of visible sound and vibration. When placing a plate of sand above a speaker and intoning a note on the musical scale through the speaker, the sand will form a specific geometric pattern for each note. We are a little late to the cymatics party as cymatic compositions have been found in such structures as the Rosslyn chapel. In the beginning was the word. Words are vibrations.

Dr. Masaru Emoto discovered that water is much more intelligent and susceptible to emotions that anyone could imagine! Dr. Emoto developed a research design with double blinds where his technicians were clueless as to the purpose and nuances of the design. Dr. Emoto took petri dishes of water, his techs slapped printed words on the petri dishes, they froze the water to make crystals and took pictures of those crystals.

Words such as love, thank you, and peace created elegant well-formed crystal of amazing beauty. Words such as hate, evil, anger created disgusting and gray crystals. How did this occur? No one in the research design put out a thought one way or the other for good or bad. How could the water imprint such higher order terms that were just written down? I think words have power. What are the limits to this train of thought? What can I change in my life with thought? Are there glass ceilings? I don't know how much control man has over his life, his destiny.

So much of our lives are predetermined by the place and time that we are born. There are statistical outliers, people like Oprah that outshine their circumstances, these are exceptions to the rules. As far as I can reckon, man is born under a star. Man's star determines his overall fortune and standing in life. One's standing is rarely malleable. You are born under a star and that is your lot in life. Miracles happen, statistical anomalies occur. However, the probability of outshining your star is rare and nearly non-existent.

The trajectory of one's life is influenced by a second great force, living luck. Living luck has a life of its own. Living luck is chimerical and difficult to pinpoint. Some are moderately lucky at love, and entirely lucky at careers etc. Living luck is a force outside of talent, hard work and merit. Some have very little talent, are meritless and are woefully deficient in applying hard work principles, yet they excel in life because they have positive living luck.

Some are born under a star of sadness, and have negative living luck. These are the forgotten and thrown away citizens, denizens of darkness. The third force that controls man's existence is the miraculous. Twists of fate have elevated and decimated man with seldom a rhyme or reason. Such is the whim of the divine.

I believe things are as they are until they are not.

"... and don't criticize what you can't understand." Bob Dylan

MH Kisner

The Great American Deception

There is a diverse and rich discussion regarding what American poverty is, who is susceptible to a life of poverty, and attrition statistics for graduates of poverty slaying programs. The litany is nearly an infinite number of ways and approaches to understanding American poverty. None of them has seemed to touch the tip of the iceberg of the mélange of issues that create and maintain poverty within an individual, a subgroup, or a caste. Herein lies the answer: Perception is everything. The person or group perceiving those in poverty come to the table with their own notions of poverty. Researchers and pundits may consider American Poverty a foreign country, which they are fascinated by on one hand, yet run away from traveling in this country like the plague.

I believe that American Poverty is *the* imminent, integral issue that pervades our nation. The failure to identify and address the American Poverty machination is and will halt all progress for America along the following axis: Education, healthcare, civil rights, America's viability as a world power, the collapsing infrastructure, our position within the global economy, and the ability to be innovative. Indeed, our threadbare grip on democratic principles relies largely upon our success or failure in challenging the mechanisms that perpetuate poverty.

Although President Johnson declared war on poverty on January 8th, 1964, few have taken to the battlefield. And no concerted battalion has been raised within our nation to slay this Quixotian dragon. Steps have been taken to mitigate the whelp of the impoverished; Food stamps, housing assistance, welfare to work, vocational training, and public service educational components have entered the foray of poverty issues within our hallowed nation. Yet, poverty persists. In pragmatic terms our failure to dissolve economic barriers can be boiled down and described in the following colloquial terms: 1. We didn't do the job as stated 2.We identified the wrong job 3.we identified the right issues and are working on it, it's just going to take more time and effort along the presently identified areas.

I have discovered a slew of anti-poverty research, policies, and programs currently being offered within America. All of them appear well intended. Most seem out of touch with both the impoverished and poverty themselves. Some are making a difference within the marginalized lives. None have identified the cause and cure of poverty within America. Poverty in America is much simpler than what the politicians, pundits, and swell of anti-poverty serviceperson would give credit to. Sadly, I have talked and teased, I have questioned and studied American poverty issues ardently for around three years. Out of all of the people the I questioned, and sources that I researched, only an august 88-year-old WWII veteran could pinpoint the core cause of American poverty. He did it with one word.

Before I divulge the sage wisdom of my aging WWII friend's assessment of the American Poverty plight, I find it incumbent upon myself to address some of the studies and programs around poverty issues. When I assimilate and assess a source I raise my attention to *what* is being said, *how* it is being said, *what is not* being said, and *who* the person or persons are that are making the statements.

In 2001 Barbara Ehrenreich did the unthinkable. She traded her comfortable middle class khakis in exchange for the blue and oft times faded denim of the working poor. Ms. Ehrenreich walked a mile in the impoverished footsteps as an underpaid and what she describes as the invisible poor. As a waitress, maid and other less glamorous labor positions she found out first hand some of the barriers to financial stability met by the working poor. Barbara was quickly immersed in the overwhelming sense of futility that her counterparts are born into.

She quickly came to the conclusion that much of a person's civil rights were parked at the door as a working and impoverished person started a work shift. For Barbara and many impoverished, work involved health risks, humiliations from fellow employees, employers, customers and the work in and of itself. She discovered how precarious one's position is in life for the poor. Health setbacks, family turmoil, legal issues that run the gamut of parking tickets to landlord/tenant agreements, transportation, and housing are only a few of the factors that affect the poor in substantially different ways than the middle or upper-class. Furthermore, Barbara worked sometimes two jobs, one full-time and another part-time yet she could not afford to maintain even a modest and off-times lugubrious apartment! Work did not work for her.

With great humility Ehrenreich discovered that many laborers with even the greatest grit could not afford to stay afloat with one full-time job, and quite often a second job did not tip the financial scales to create financial freedom. Very few policymakers that act within the American poverty forum have tread where she has trod. Very few state governors, congressmen, or federal cabinet members have felt the deprivations, insecurities and hardships that Ehrenreich and her blue-collar ilk have felt. And why is that? Wasn't our nation founded by farmers, ink stained journalists/publishers, and common folk?

Ehrenreich revisits her seminal work of *Nickel and Dimed* in her 2008 tome *This Land is Their Land*. *This Land is Their Land* is comprised of pithy essays and vignettes of the ludicrous and unscrupulous abuses plied against the poor via private and non-profit greed. It appears that by 2008 Ehrenreich's understanding of poverty issues has deepened and broadened to understand the greater complexities of daily life for the poor. There is no single cure for poverty. Ehrenreich's tone of writing and style has become more acerbic and less tolerant of the institutional and class created obstacles that the American poor face.

This Land is Their Land illuminates the abyss that separates the haves from the have-nots. If *Nickel and Dimed* was a study of the pervading futility laid before the impoverished. *This Land is Their Land* points out some of the major players and their different set of rules than those that they oppressed. Examples of failed CEO's receiving enormous salaries and perks whilst they bring their companies to ruin smack in the face of the atrocities that the working poor are dealt with for absurd infractions such as forgetting to bring sugar substitute to a table that they are waiting on.

LIBERTY

One cannot read *This Land is Their Land* without being infuriated with not only the ruling caste, but also the system that upholds their immoral ways. Like our nation, *This Land is Their Land* is a vision of stark contrast. We have accepted this contrast without question. There are many subtexts, which interweave within the non-verbal panorama of American Poverty and class. The finger of responsibility can be rightfully pointed at a sundry of certain people and situations. One significant factor that has perpetuated poverty in America is the control of the middle class.

The bell-curve demonstrates the few rich, positive outliers are to be far ahead of the pack. They are insulated from the middle-class world, and even more so separated from the world of the poor. The middle and industrious hump of the bell curve is filled with the masses, the great populace of the middle class. These are those that have dreams. The middle-class have nice homes albeit modest. Those of the middle are gainfully employed working on career ladders, vacations, college funds, and an occasional round of golf or night out. The middle class is more or less satiated. The fact that the middle class is satiated and full of hope is pre-eminent. Herein lies the lynchpin to poverty.

The middle-class has hope, they see some fruits of their labor. And labor to them, is the key to contentment. The poor just need to get a job. The blind spots of the middle class are: 1. Just because they have been offered a financially sound career track doesn't mean that an impoverished person with the same training will receive the same equitable opportunity or advancement. 2. The middle-class fails to see that inequity is designed to be constant. 3. The middle-class fails to see how and where they individually and collectively perpetuate inequity. 4. The middle-class, like their upper-class counterparts fail to see, to understand, and address the very real psychosocial, and physical gestalt of poverty. There are two groups in America, the wealthy and the poor; neither knows how the other lives.

Researcher and author Beth Shulman tackles the issue of the working poor in her opus, *The Betrayal of Work*. Shulman cuts right to the chase by stating "Indeed, our recent prosperity rests, in part, on their misery..." (2003). Shulman identifies a multitude of erroneous assumptions that the middle and upper classes perpetuate about the American poor. The failure to comprehend the impossible circumstances that the impoverished are dealt with is endemic amongst all current research that I have come across. How can Americans be oblivious to the circumstances and people who build and clean their homes? When a limping waitress brings a plate of food to them, what occurs between a middle class person's earlobes to not be curious or aware of the plight of their fellow citizens?

Shulman's work seems to go hand in hand with Ehrenreich's contributions to the topic of American poverty. Shulman delves deeper into the filial issues that are often neglected within poor topics. Impoverished families have extra marks against them compared to their middle class counterparts. Most impoverished families are led by single mother's struggling to get by, erstwhile their children are often left to fend for themselves. The lugubrious constellation of environmental influences paints a sad picture for impoverished families, especially children. Poor unhealthy housing, violence riddled communities, sub-par school systems, there are many roads leading to poverty, yet very few leading out of the cursed impoverished state.

My wife earned her Master's in Education within a cohort of fellow students. The class was asked if they would be willing to forgo a computer in their child's school so that it could be given to an under-funded elementary school that had a large impoverished population. One of my wife's colleagues was reticent to donate an imaginary computer to help out another school or child other than her own. This student cited a concern that her child may lose out on an educational opportunity if a computer was rerouted to another school. Let's back up. I wonder how many of my wife's cohorts were secretly agreeing with this outspoken minority. How many people within this class would pull the lever and vote for withholding a computer in their child's school secretly, anonymously?

The wayward student and future educator developed her premise as follows: My child comes first, the other school community has the responsibility to provide for their own, and I will outspokenly advocate for the opportunities of my child to be intact and not marginalized or reduced. On one hand, I commend her for speaking her voice, to be frank and candid. Subterfuge is not outspoken…it stabs you in the back while you are not looking. Subterfuge persuades you to believe or keep your focus on point A whilst a concerted effort to your demise is planned and executed. I think this student has a promising career within education, especially if she has learned the finer points of subterfuge.

I immediately identified the visceral and omniscient drive of self-preservation within this future educator's heuristic. One common thread that the poor, middle and upper class share is the need to survive. The need to survive trumps the pleasantries of a society of rules, laws, and due process. Beyond and behind the façade of humanity's social contract lies the prime operative: Survive and thrive at all costs. When a congressman plays dirty politics and wiretaps his opponents for information, he is only doing what he was born to do; create an uneven playing field that will give himself and his kin the advantage. When a local police officer blatantly breaks the civil or criminal law on duty or off duty that he has sworn to protect and uphold he is only doing what he was born to do; create an uneven playing field that will give himself and his kin the advantage. Unfair advantage is the key to maintaining poverty. Subterfuge in creating relative satiety, and believing in equality and nearly boundless opportunity is the vehicle for carrying out the caste system.

David Shipler adds to the cacophony of author-researchers who have identified a malignant polyp on humanity's back, namely impoverished workers. Shipler (2004) fills out the dismal picture of working poor people's inability to gain recognition, basic healthcare, civil rights and a departure from the bane of poverty by the sweat of their brow. Conversely, Shipler points out that their very employment with some companies and situations diminishes their capacity to feel self-effacious and liberated. My World War II veteran friend posited that America does not have a poverty problem, it has a wealth and greed problem.

I believe the best ways to make time fly are to send your kids to school and throw a clock out a window.

LIBERTY

August 14, 2011

Dear Joe and Rosa,

At times I truly get lost in thought. At times like this, clarity seems so far away. From beginning to end, life appears to be a riddle. I foolishly attempt to understand large concepts and large systems as they relate to small behaviors.

The one truth that I have found is that the actions from people espousing large and noble ideas are often incongruent with their behavior. For instance, the modern education system has been structured upon an ageless and august commitment to humane ideals. Namely, all people can and should be literate. More recently, people from all walks of life can improve upon their station in life through education.

This incongruency arises out of workplace discrimination, irresponsible capitalism, a failure to provide true checks and balances within education, government, and capitalist systems, and the hoarding of money by the few whom also oppress the poor in wages.

"Seeing into darkness is clarity" Tao Te Ching

Forever Yours,

Hermes Trismegistus (AKA Hermes)

Songs: *Come Together*, **The Beatles**
Get Together, **The Youngbloods**

On *Not* Taking Care Of Business

How can one work and be impoverished? Isn't one job a foot-in-the-door experience for a rich and rewarding career track? After making one's bones in a low-paying job isn't one promoted upon merit and hard work? Our federal, state, municipal, and private sector organizations have created algorithms, programs and practices in place to lift people out of poverty through work related incentives. These impoverished people don't pay taxes, or if they do...their tax rate is so low compared to mine the wealthy, that there is no excuse for them to be where they are!!!

Should one be so jejune to accept such premises that deride or descry the impoverished, then they truly have not experienced the other life being lived in America. I was enrolled in a doctoral program that followed the cohort paradigm. One of my colleagues was aghast and nearly traumatized that Kmart started carrying Craftsman tools. To her, Kmart was socially beneath the quality and reputation of Craftsman, she still hasn't recovered. When talking about the impoverished, my colleague just could not fathom why the poor didn't just pull themselves up by their bootstraps. The consensus amongst my colleagues was nearly unanimous. I disagreed. I argued that most of the American poor don't have boots or bootstraps.

To highlight the plight of the American poor I lent this fellow student and future policymaker a book with the injunction to read the author penned introduction and explanation regarding the sensitive issues, content, and style being addressed in the book *The Beans of Egypt, Maine.* This book follows the historical fiction life of poor peoples within rural America. *The Beans of Egypt, Maine* is a dismal and lugubrious account of major themes and events that occur within poor rural American communities. Along with the injunction of caution, I quipped to my classmate after reading this tome you may understand that oft-times Americans don't have boots or bootstraps.

Upon returning this book, my classmate was speechless and nearly in shock. Some moments in your life are turning points and will forever haunt you such as the exchange of her returning the book to me as I stated "Now you know a little bit about my childhood...some of my struggles." I must table the deeper exploration of how that moment changed my life until later in this work. At this juncture the primary thought to come away with is being aware of how disparate and out-of touch the educational elite and future policymakers are to the stark realities of the poor...and the more global thread of how the mismanagement of poverty is causing our society's demise. *"Living is easy with eyes closed, misunderstanding all you see..."* Strawberry Fields, The Beatles.

More recently, a retirement age couple awoke to the blight around them. Not whilst they were raising a family, or building equity in a home, or enjoying one of many vacations. Rather, this couple received a calling from "God" just as they were retiring. Personally, I liken them to Saul on the road to Damascus, who after years of skewering the downtrodden, had a change of heart and habits wipes their former transgressions clean.

That being said, David and Liane Phillips deserve great accolades for tirelessly devoting their retirement years to the poor within their community. First and foremost, although there are many well-deserving people throughout the world, charity begins at home. And charity, kindness, and advocacy is much needed within our own backyard. Robust kudos to the Phillips for their undying effort. After reading Liane and her co-author Echo Montgomery's report on their pet project Cincinnati Works, I am not entirely convinced that the authors have digested other researcher's experiences such as Ehrenreich, Shulman, or Shipler.

LIBERTY

It wasn't until retirement age that David Shipler had a fleeting glimpse into why some of the urban African-American community is wary of law-enforcement. I don't want to sling-mud or minimalize the Phillips' contribution to the Cincinnati community and the national attention to poverty issues. Truly, we need people from their caste to join us in the battle regarding poverty issues. I just wish that they invested more time of their life in the trenches with their poor brethren.

Regardless, the Cincinnati Works is a holistic model of finding and retaining entry-level jobs that offer health care for the poor. Again, employment seems to be the panacea or prescription for poverty. Ten years into the program, it's declared a success, retention is high, welfare rolls are low. By the way, after ten years of the programs inception employee advancement is non-existent, and the participants for all intents and purposes are still impoverished with no clear way out of the shackles of their caste.

Cincinnati Works provides a plethora of services that the working poor would not have access to otherwise. Basic legal services, simple social work, coaching, counseling, and an essential feeling of having an extended family with the staff members are provided gratis to diligent clients…er "members." Giving jobseekers the moniker of "member" appears warm and friendly, maybe even inviting, it's a clarion call for being a responsible stakeholder on one hand, yet on the other hand it smacks of the non-union brainwashing espoused by Wal-Mart and greatly exposed and derided by Ehrenreich (2008).

Truly Cincinnati Works has its heart in the right place! The workers and volunteer personnel *are* making a difference in many people's lives. Is it the right direction and paradigm for the American impoverished? I am not entirely convinced that it is. I was once told by a sage that you can't kill a lion by cutting off its tail. Maybe the Cincinnati Works paradigm is feeding the lion. Maybe finding entry-level work for the indigent solves little to none.

Author-researcher Philip Devol, Et. Al. remind us that in 1999, well before the great recession of 2008, 42% of workers were considered poor. Jobs are not providing the means to overcome the condition of poverty. Devol, Et. Al. suggest that the middle class is shrinking (Devol, P., Et. Al., 2006, p. viii). What would be the fallout of the shrinking of the middle class? Will the middle class reconnoiter the thankless minimum wage jobs from their historically impoverished counterparts? Consider the fact that the net worth of the top 10% income earners' is $833,600 compared, to that of their impoverished bottom 20%'s net worth of $7,900 (Devol, P., Et. Al., 2006, p. viii). What are the differences in opportunity along education, health care, recreation, personal growth, political representation and overall happiness in comparing the lives of the rich and poor? Devol et. Al. argue that in the 1940's companies paid 33% of all tax monies collected in the U.S. compared to citizen contribution of 44%. In the 1990's companies are said to contribute 14% of all taxes collected, and citizens contribute 73% of all taxes collected.

Of all of the policymakers and prevalent author researchers that I have come across, none seem to identify two major threads that create and perpetuate poverty. Poverty is often identified as a problem in and of itself, an obscure aberration of society. By even the most well intended politician and humanitarian, poverty is a metastasized polyp amongst us to be eradicated. Scholars and well doers strive to pinpoint and label the complexities of American poverty. Tangled webs of behavioral and organic inputs weave in and out of the discussion of urban poverty, rural poverty, multigenerational poverty, educational interventions, vocational interventions, healthcare, substance abuse, gender studies, and minority studies are only a few stops on the perpetual ride that politicians, pundits, well-doers and academicians pursue. The discussion within these sub-communities is dizzying. Never mind bringing these pundits and advocates together to create a lasting change within our hallowed country. Heck, very few of these spokespeople agree on what poverty is.

I propose that poverty is not the problem. Poverty is a symptom of a greater issue. Since the dawn of humanity's time the concept of poverty has remained static. As tribes, nations, and peoples have arisen from the dust, they have done so upon the backs of a lower caste. Call them slaves, wage slaves, serfs, indentured servants… the names and faces change but the concept remains the same. The sweat of Pharaoh's brow did not build the pyramids at Giza. Neither are the great roads, buildings and temples of today's society built by the Pharaonic caste.

"Well, the world needs ditch diggers too!" Was not forwarded by anyone who has seriously dug ditches by hand, for low pay. This glib statement does more to perpetuate the abuse of another man's life than what we normally give credence to. Poverty is symptomatic of a few, financially elite exploiting those behind and below him. American capitalism is a pyramid scheme gone amok. In recent years, there have been CEO's that earn up to 500% more than the minimum wage, and still lead their companies into financial ruin. So much for the term merit pay, adios to our long held belief in work incentive for ingenuity, accountability, and other performance based ideologies!

There is no problem with poverty, at least from the upper caste's perspective. After all, if you are poor, just get a job, dig a ditch. Why is the economic divide between the upper 10% and the bottom 30% of income earners so vast, so lopsided? The answer is simple, because we allow it. America has a wealth problem.

There is writing on the wall, a clarion call whispered between the working poor in low lit, low paying workplace break rooms. There is a hungry wail within the hearts of over 60 million impoverished Americans. The deafening and primal scream encapsulated within the economically forgotten demands freedom and liberation from the shackles of poverty and all that poverty entails. Even the most economically insulated, and financially well fed must hear the reverberating echo of what our failed society has created and continues to perpetuate.

Associated Press reporter Hope Yen encapsulates the failed American tradition of poverty in her two recent articles *Census: 1 in 7 Americans Live in Poverty,* and *Census Finds Record Gap Between Rich and Poor.* For both of these articles journalist Yen discusses poverty according to the national standard of having $21, 954 annual income per household of four people. After deductions, (yes, the poor pay taxes too!), what once was a sneeze away from $22K income becomes about 17K per year income for four people!

It should not take a group of Yale educated policymakers to realize that $22K is an abysmal number and benchmark for poverty. Meanwhile the median American income per household was and is falling from $50,000 per year. Certainly, the number of households struggling with life, the loss of the American dream, and the failure of the American promise is greater than one in seven. Households that bring in $40K a year for a family of four are still in a financially precarious position. Numbers hang on the tapestry of our society like stalwart chameleons, numbers are there yet they hide tales that have lives of their own.

An American chameleon is the disproportionate number of people within America that struggle and barely survive at the $40k per year level. Life is kind of acceptable at this point; we're not rich but there is a present or two under the Christmas tree. Traditionally we have an annual family portrait taken and an albeit modest vacation. Whoopsi-doodle! The American dollar is losing value… We have to make our dollars stretch. Vacation turns into stay-cation. Life doesn't become horrible until we start losing our jobs and homes. Now where do we go from here? The chameleon of our culture…, which has always been present, is: The rich get richer, and the poor get poorer. The dummy game is to keep enough people in the middle content, satiated, anesthetized to the reality. Economic fluctuations of bull and bear markets etc. rarely faze the impoverished. They have no 401k's, 529's, mortgage ARM's, they have no boots nor do they have boot-straps. Recessions and inflation etc. rarely topple the affluents' apple cart. Investments and investors usually huddle and merely change their game plan during recessions and the like.

Recessions and eras of inflation help keep the middle class in check. Should the middle become too affluent, the absence of their work and services would create a gaping hole in the American fabric. Shortages of middle class labor occur, albeit fleeting. In the present quandary, the middle class is feeling the pinch. Should the market improve, the worst will happen. Namely, life will go back to normal for Americans. Should the historically middle class market follow it's current trajectory, a splendid thing will occur, namely a revolution.

There are more chameleons hanging on the wall; few people notice them or care much about them. States such as Mississippi follow woefully behind in poverty at 23.1% compared to states such as New Hampshire citing a lowly 7.8% poverty rate (Yen, 2010). Minorities are still most likely to be hit hard by poverty with 25.3% of Hispanics living at or below $21,954 per year; 25.8% of blacks live at or below the poverty line. Whites are feeling the pinch of poverty with a disproportionate 9.4% (Yen, 2010). Somewhere, somehow the American dream has turned into a nightmare for minorities. The failure to provide greater employment equality for minorities 40 years after the Civil Rights movement is morally repugnant. Jimi Hendrix's voice rings too true *I Don't Live Today*.

The ugliest chameleon in the room is that the rich are getting richer! The wealthy few earn 49.4% of all money made in America compared to the numerous poor that earn a paltry 3.4% of America's economy (Yen, 2010). The Gini index contends that we are seeing an all-time high for income disparity since tracking rich-poor income disparity in 1967 (Yen, 2010). The wealthiest 5% added slightly to their incomes, while families with median incomes of $50,000 slipped lower. Professor Sheldon Danziger sums up a core problem, "We're pretty good about not talking about income inequality." (Yen, 2010).

Although the rife of defining what poverty is continues, the poor know it most intimately. Poverty is a pervading reality of futility; work doesn't work. Going to school for advanced degrees does not always equate to freedom from poverty. Even with a solid job placement, impoverished graduates are mostly strapped with high levels of student loans, closed career doors if they are not insiders and come without the robust high rolling employment references that those who have a network of family and friends have. After all, one hand washes another with career advancement. Transcending poverty through entrepreneurship and further education is possible, just grossly improbable in America.

The middle class continues to beat the drum of freedom from the shackles of poverty through work, more work, and even more work. Meanwhile the middle class is oblivious to the different set of rules and faux opportunities proffered to the under-class than those nearly inherent opportunities and road rules that they own. The importance of middle-class satiation cannot be over-emphasized. So long as the middle is content, there is no reason for their great numbers to rise up and effect change within the American forum. Life is good. However, should the American middle be pressured to see, to accept the fact that equality is a platitude and its resources reserved for the few, and then revolution would be afoot. The tenuous and fleeting power remains within the elites' hands. The elite control policy, they can throw away scraps to acquiesce the middle class and when necessary, the impoverish. The power to affect change and revolution does not belong to the impoverished, statistically they are too few.

The poor have little strength or where-withal to storm the Bastille. Should the poor become insurgent by themselves, their efforts will be squashed by the numerous middle-class. Its only the growing discontent and rise to malcontent of the middle-class will revolution occur. And it's happening. The current financial economic peril that the middle class is facing teeters upon barely content to awakening to reality. The big dummy game, the poorly played pyramid scheme. American Capitalism is a dog-eat-dog hierarchy. For centuries we have hidden behind the disguise of American supremacy of lifestyle, education, industry etc... however, karma states that all roosters will come home to roost and it's nigh twilight upon the American Capitalist stage.

In the 1970's America faced a recession. The recession of the 1970's was felt and lived by the greatest generation. The generation that witnessed the evil of tyranny abroad, faced it, and conquered it. America recovered and seemingly strengthened. The speck of evil that existed within America from it's inception through the 1970's was tolerable and mitigated by other strengths. America and Americans could still boast of it's industry. Low paid workers had greater stability and commitment from their employers, they experienced less turmoil and uncertainty from job turnover turmoil as we do now. There was a nostalgia of quality; A pride in micro-community and macro-nationalistic community. We were mostly proud of our leaders and the system, which we existed in.

A new day dawned within our society. Dishonest, disloyal leaders filled the seats of our sacred government. Somewhere, something happened... America transitioned from being the land of the many to the land of the few. Our foreign policy changed. On the wake of the World Wars we injudiciously chose to enter skirmishes based upon faulty reasoning. The Bay of Pigs, Guatemala, North Korea, Vietnam, The Gulf Wars, our confusing history with Afghanistan, and the Israel-Palestinian-American political triad to name a few American hoary and confusing war-mongering ventures.

The American dream evaporated. No more could a family rely upon loyalty, hardwork, honest and equitable processes in America; these are no longer American values. The community died. The American family died. The death of family dinners, of game night, of single income houses perished. The Savior of the American way is silent. The core problem is the lack of equitable opportunity to life affirming resources.

Financial opportunity, stability lacking within impoverished and increasingly middle class lives, quality of life (healthcare, diet, time to rest, etc.), the right and opportunity to family, and quality innovative education are all missing within our dying society. All of the afore mentioned items depend upon financial freedom for all citizens. True financial freedom creates authentic democracy. Without financial freedom for all citizens, the reins of government will perpetually and solely belong to those that have.

One of the saddest themes that I have witnessed on the stage of life occurred within a county courtroom. I was at the courtroom fighting a seatbelt infraction. There were about 20 other fellow citizens there that day. Nearly all of them were in attendance due to loud mufflers. The county had a prosecutor in attendance that would offer "lowered" charges. In exchange for reportable violations on one's driving record, or worse the full fine available to the magistrate's pen, the prosecutor would meet with the accused beforehand and offer "deals". The deals consisted of fines around $200-$400 per person. My soul wept that day.

Here is the zenith of our democratic heritage. Here are the benefits birthed by the sacrifice and frequently supreme sacrifice of our servicemen. Here is democracy at it's worse. Here is the abuse of power only acknowledged by the downtrodden. The law states… Who made the law? Your congressional representative…What does he or she know about loud mufflers? Right…if I worked harder I wouldn't have a loud muffler…ok. Who is the law enforcer? What background does he or she have? Are they really fighting crime by targeting and issuing so many loud muffler citations? Who are the people getting loud muffler citations? Hmmm…Not my congressmen… a couple of factory workers but no police officers…hmmm? What forms of due process are truly available and accessible to those receiving loud muffler citations?

All 18 or 20 of those citizens pleaded guilty and received a "deal". I pleaded not guilty and fought my ticket at a later date. Being without means, I did the foolish thing and represented myself. Rule number one to navigating the American judiciary system: Always find an attorney that is on first name basis with the judge or magistrate…preferably an attorney that T's off or belongs to the same social circle of the magistrate. Drawing upon dense research of perception, observation, science theories such as the Arrow of Time, and dusty-forgotten clauses of our legal system; I was victorious in my defense! Is the system accessible to the average layperson? No. The Democratic process is suspended for those that have not.

Very few people have truly tackled the issue of economic disparity and poverty in America. From where I am sitting, impoverished and middle class Americans fair about as well along financial planes as the French under Marie Antoinette's rule. What good is it to balk of being a leading humanistic nation when such a schism in race and income equity parallels that of authoritarian, monarchial, or communist nations?

Empty platitudes fill the void where fundamental change is required. Was America founded by farmers, spiritual dissidents, and colossal humanists only to sink into a nation governed solely by the wealthy? Is the current American dream slipping away, only to be replaced by a perdurable and oppressive caste system?

Where can we find the economic and lifestyle intentions-expectations of our noble and august American founders? What needs to happen to create a lasting change along economic opportunity axis within America? How can we stop this poorly played have-have-not dummy game that has plagued humanity from it's inception? Is it beyond our ability to create a truly equitable society? Is it possible to create a social contract that does not oppress another in word, deed, or interpretation or are we truly animals growling over a half-chewed bone; the lot of our daily existence?

Maybe, deep down we know. Maybe we know the higher road to take in order to right the wrongs developed and perpetuated through our low-middle-high class (caste) system that is the blight of our union. Maybe the voice of reason will not and cannot be found on a golf course, a posh resort, or a swanky fundraiser dinner.

Maybe the voice of reason; the next American Revolution and revolutionaries can be found right where the original founding fathers sprouted. Maybe the right person for the right job isn't groomed at an elite private school. Perhaps the next American Revolution is in the air now. Whispered on the lips of the forgotten within dank, lugubrious, and earthy pubs.

I believe that if you always do as you did, you will always get as you got.

Our Long And Windy Road

Plans are made for the next day. We all go to sleep quickly. We sleep like logs. Morning comes and brings a hearty appetite for everyone in our party. We head down stairs to the hotel restaurant. Pancakes, no syrup, for Steph. A shared side of pancakes and bacon for the boys. Grandpa orders a three egg, three bacon, three-pancake meal. Eggs, biscuits and gravy for me. The waitress is a thin short gal in her 50's and she is serving for the entire restaurant. Coffee cups are empty, finished families tap their bill impatiently against the table, and we wait.

Our meal takes close to an hour to arrive. No drink refills for us, our meal was fine even though you didn't ask. I feel bad for this lady...this is a job for two or three people. The owners must be skinflints. Who knows, maybe our waitress scared away the last busboys and waitresses. It's a riddle. All roads lead to Wal-Mart, and so our heels turn to this megalithic retail chain. I try not to think about it, about Wal-Mart's failures to take care of their own via unions, health insurance and a livable wage.

Ida is my first stop. I attuned her to Reiki III shortly before our exodus from the south. Ida is a sweet country lady that takes pride in only ever being with one man, her husband of 36 years. Ida spends vast amounts of time with her two grandsons, she likes to garden and cook. Ida is a little redheaded lady that is often set in her ways and unassuming. I enjoy Ida's company because what you see is what you get, no more and no less.

Ida and I exchange Reiki for over two hours. We talk, and she feeds me, missing my children but still somewhat engaged in the conversation. We both affirm our friendship, wish that we lived closer, and promise to stay in touch. Much of the day is now spent. I jump on my motorcycle, careful not to re-burn my leg on the muffler. I head to the outskirts of town where a dear friend Susan Host lives. Susan is a sustainable lifestyle guru. Susan is a student of world history. Susan sees the writing on the wall with our economy, our lifestyles, our over-dependence on foreign oil or any petroleum product. Susan is a seer, she peers into our future and realizes that we cannot go on like this for long, we are at the end of our rope. Susan and I are both cogently aware that American freedom is disappearing, democracy has not fully been achieved in our land and is posed to do an about face.

Susan and I are kindred spirits, not only because of our philosophical bent and propensity to love all things living, we've met like this sometime before. Maybe we had a past life, maybe we meet in our dreams, maybe we are both entirely lost in that ephemeral and Elysian mist that weighs heavily upon a seer's brow.

I've gone to the wrong gate and I don't realize it yet. I should have gone to the normal gate that I used to enter. Susan has animals that roam, the gates keep their road hungry souls safe. Moreover, Susan is just as happy living on her farm, no need to stray outside. All she wants and needs is here. How contrary to our over consumption society! I feel like a putz because I went in the wrong gate. Susan puts me at ease with a bear hug befitting a man four times her petite and pretty frame. It's nice to be loved, to have friends.

We meander and talk in broken sentences as we feed this animal, and water that one. I love farms, and I am head over heels for hers!

Susan raises her animals with the right mixture of love, compassion and practicality. The farm exudes life and I bask in the rays of love and life. Turkey drakes follow us curiously, impishly half-pecking me, trying and testing me...*who is this new guy?* Susan and I sit down in yard chairs, and one of her favorite toms lands on her lap as she peers over its healthy body to finish her sentence, I chuckle.

Our conversation quickly leaps from small talk and the pedestrian to a state-of-affairs coverage of our economy, our freedoms, our government, our quality of life. Time stops as her golden blonde hair glows in the afternoon light. In an hour's time, I have sat at the feet of a sage, a priestess of golden knowledge. We promise to stay in touch. I don't fear the future, yet I have a strong heavy feeling in my gut. I leave the gates of paradise renewed, yet with this oversized weight in my gut. This is my passion, this farm, our freedoms, our future.

Time drifts through an hourglass, and there is never enough time for friends. That evening finds me at Diane's house. Diane is the quintessential sweetheart. A brunette with two grown daughters, and a very kind husband. Diane has opened her home for a large Reiki exchange that drags on to 10pm. I could never imagine Diane being mad, or her feathers even ruffled. Diane is grace incarnated. The full moon penetrates the window and shines light upon our lives and healing work.

The wife is irate when I return to the hotel. The boys are zonked. Instead of a protracted argument, we opt to go to sleep. Morning comes entirely too early, we pack up. It seems we make a dozen trips toting our stuff downstairs. Stephanie is again the car top carrier stuffer. Tom packs the back of the car. I pack my motorcycle, and bring all things downstairs whilst watching the boys. We have many miles to travel today. Good, I need to move far away from here as the ghosts draw in closer around me. I cannot look these malevolent and disembodied spirits in the eye; I am afraid of what I will see.

Sunscreen slides up and down my body, my dew rag needs a good washing as it is damp and heavy with sweat. Anxious to peel out of here, anxious to move away from a grave calling me just seven miles south.

I lead the way and peel rubber up and over the mountain pass. Down 81 south, there is a slow-down, a virtual parking lot south of Harrisonburg...and we wait. *Rode in on a greyhound, guess I'll be walking out if I go...* The stereo is acting up again... I thump it three times... more out of exasperation than thinking something would actually stop it. However, it did stop and I was relieved. I let Tom and Steph know that I was pulling off for gas, and to join me at the next exit.

We'll follow route 11 for twenty miles around the traffic and hop back on, follow me was my injunction to them when we met at the gas station. The boys ask for another store bought drink, a prank they would pull at nearly every pit stop on grandpa for the remainder of the trip. I smirk.

On 81 south now, headed for Atlanta. In my undergraduate studies I saw a documentary with Dr. Martin Luther King Jr. featured in it. This documentary had actual footage of Dr. King's address to the cadre of supporters he had outside his home shortly after it was bombed. His family was supposed to be in the home, it was a quirk of nature, a miracle that his family was spared. On the front steps, the only discernable feature to an otherwise decimated home. Dr. King assuaged his followers' wrath and appetite for retribution by telling them, not this way, not by violence. I had to paraphrase Dr. King's comments here as it has been many years since I had seen this footage.

I told my sister that I wanted to travel to the Dr. King home. She giggled "are you serious?" She was incredulous that I would want to pay homage to King's lasting legacy, which hurt me. It hurt me that my sister didn't see the need to fully participate and appreciated such a spiritual giant amidst our American fabric. It hurt me that she did not realize the importance of Dr. King's work, which carried over into the women's rights movement. But then again, I am the younger brother. The march into Atlanta by General Sherman was also a pivotal moment during the Civil War. General Sherman burned and pillaged a path to Atlanta. Sherman fed and supplied his soldiers from the pantries of southern people in lieu of having his own supply train. Sherman's march on Atlanta struck fear into the Confederates' hearts, demolished the confederates' military lines, and was an overall victory for the North. Had Sherman not taken Atlanta, the North may not have had the momentum to win further battles. The outcome of the Civil War may have been drastically different. Ergo, the progress and accomplishments of Dr. King and the civil rights movement may never had occurred. To me, Atlanta is a crossroads of liberty. I must go to Atlanta.

We didn't make it to Atlanta that day. Evening found us entering Pigeon Forge, North Carolina. Pigeon Forge is a wonderful vacation resort town. There are dinner-theatres, mini-golf galore, Dollyland, helicopter tours, comedy clubs and much more. We were now in the Great Smoky Mountains. The mountains loomed twenty miles in front of us. Tom was ready to pull over to a campground along the strip in Pigeon Forge. No way! I said through my helmet. I want to camp there! Pointing at the dark looming mountains ahead. So we made tracks, darkness fell and we were in the middle of the mountains looking for a campground.

Exhausted and in ill humor from hard monotonous riding, we pulled over to a closed visitor's center to study a map outside on a kiosk. A sundry of moths, flies, and other winged bugs flit and fly into the lit kiosk. There were paper maps compliments of the National Park Service. Tom and I argued as to which way was up; finally Tom threw the map on the ground, "Fine! We'll do it your way!" No, I don't want to, I added not willing to be responsible. I led in the direction that Tom proposed. Sure enough, I was wrong! We ended up at the Elkmont campground a little after 9pm.

The campground was crowded, and cars lined the paved loops with sparse trees and vegetation. One campsite melded into another. Car doors opened and slammed shut in concert. Campers beeped themselves in and out of their cars with their keep fobs. Trunks opened mystically on their own, trunk lights filled the night in between car lights flashing on and off as campers remembered one last needful item to go to sleep with. Our campsite sprung up in the dark, wordless and nearly effortless as we had created a routine. The boys played quietly, a few trips to and from the bathroom found us ready to sleep.

LIBERTY

Hermes and I regained our vigil staring at the starry sky. We were both eager to avoid certain topics: Sanity, the horror of the shallow grave left behind in Luray without even a marker to commemorate the poor lost soul, and of course our culpability with respect to those dreary times. Hermes and I know and collude that these mountains are ancient, mystical and hold the secrets of yesteryear. Orbs speckle the night sky; I greet our far away neighbors and invite them to come down in their ultra fangled spaceships. Our thoughts turn towards tomorrow, will we make it to Atlanta? How can we commemorate Dr. King's legacy? How can we pay homage to the troubled yet triumphant march on Atlanta by General Sherman? How can we keep the wife, kids and grandpa appeased in the 105 degree Atlanta heat? Mulling compromises, options, changes in gear.

It's a restless night on the mountain for me. The Smoky Mountains are rife with an arcane energy. This energy seems to change me, somehow…deep down I am one with the mountain, a neophyte initiate into its mysteries. Morning found us taking brief walks around the paved campground and then quickly tearing down the mountain at a frightening pace, especially on motorcycle as I mastered each corner. We pulled over half a dozen times for quick photo shots of imposing gorges and towering mountain ranges. Grandpa was especially gleeful at having one foot in North Carolina and another in Tennessee. Other pilgrims pulled over to worship the beauty in similar ways.

A beautiful cool day to travel through the Great Smoky Mountains lay ahead of us. We pulled over in Cherokee, North Carolina for gas and snacks. Stephanie and I both wished that we could sightsee here, shop the wonderful Native gift stores, go through the museums. I make a solemn vow to bring my clan back here to more fully appreciate the sites and spirit that is here.

Miles flew by as our road straightened and flattened before us. The flora and fauna changed, red dirt emerged, the heat poured over us like it never had before. Our ride was broken intermittently by pit stops, quick refills and restroom breaks. Spirit indicated "E", a near failure upon a mountain with nowhere to go but down and out from the highway. No gas station could be found within 10 miles. We returned to the highway and made tracks another fifteen miles to a gas station, a close call.

What is empty, soon becomes full. What is up, must come down. What is full, becomes empty again. So goes the universe. Sparse population led us to more population. Entering the greater Atlanta area brought more traffic, more exits, more buildings, more people. Finally the traffic became so thick that the inevitable occurred; a slow down, then a virtual parking lot. Sweat poured off my brow under my helmet. Again, I feel quite martial…military-like I am riding my white horse, my helmet, my declaration in Hebrew upon my garments, and a profound conviction within my being.

I am here to add my soul's voice and vote to that which mankind has striven for since the dawn of time. I am here for humanity. I am here to fight if with no one other than the invisible demons that pock our society and threaten to destroy the rights of man. At times I feel like Don Quixote, riding a donkey and fighting windmills. At times I feel quite insane. At times I feel like I am nearly the only sane one in existence.

I fight for freedom. Because freedom is worth fighting for. I fight for freedom, because tyranny does not need a foe, tyranny relies upon the ignorant and/or complacent. Tyranny argues that things are the best they can be. Tyranny says don't rock the boat, because there are those worse off. Tyranny vehemently argues that there is nothing wrong! There is nothing wrong with the institution of slavery! There is nothing wrong with women not having the right to vote, or the right to own property! Tyranny demands that there is nothing wrong with having a ruling class of people that oppress the working class in wages, in education, in quality of life! There is nothing to see here, keep moving! Keep working. Keep tottering along in underpaid positions that do not pay living wages...this is noble!

So we are ruled by this insane stoic ethic. Einstein defined insanity as the act of doing the same thing over and over again and expecting a different outcome. Over and over again, Americans submit themselves to the powers that be, largely corporate America and the capitalist system hoping against hope that a different outcome *will* occur. This different outcome can be phrased as the American dream; home ownership, quality rest time, a basic standard of living. This goal is becoming more and more daunting to obtain. The American dream has become a chimerical and Quixotian fantasy!

Equality has never truly been the goal of the powers that be. Equality does not generate a lower working class to carry the lion's share of work requisite to keep the elite, in the elite. Endearing terms such as "For the people, by the people" are just propaganda. As my elitist doctoral professor reminded me ad nauseum "the world always needs ditch-diggers." It's been my experience that those who draw upon this adage have dug very few ditches.

The time is fast approaching where Americans and beyond will understand that it is neither necessary nor noble to always be oppressed by a few elite. The promise of a better tomorrow, of the American dream will be understood for what it is; a lie to invoke patriotism and subjectivity. The elite have always had a secret equation. This equation sums in part: Supply, demand, fear, satiety, urgency, outside threats, and noble propaganda. A witch's brew is created within their demonic cauldron of politics, contrived wars, and well-placed media propaganda. This concoction is at times force fed to us, and at other times slipped into our diet innocuously; The rape of the many; the poor.

LIBERTY

Roadside Reflections

How can I rise above just ranting about these truths? How can a poor ignorant yutz like myself create lasting change? I don't have answers. I only have questions. My questions lie upon the tracks laid before me by Pirsig. What is a *quality* filled life. My questions lie upon our forefathers' foundation to *create a more perfect union*. My questions are in the air of Gandhi's and Dr. King's last breath...*free the people*. Yet, I am quite immobile to do so. Thrashing rises up from Spirit's speakers, then a tinny guitar lick, and a voice of profound melancholia permeates all that is: *hold my breathe as I wish for death, oh God please wake me!...I cannot live, I cannot die...* I weep under the cover of my helmet. I weep for the futility of life. The error of trying. Effort is the first step on the road to failure. I weep at the profound sadness of losing a shooting star such as Dr. King; prophet of peace.

Demons encircle me, I wince closing my eyes and fighting them off with feigned strength. My shoulders and head bounce and shrug releasing their grip from me. I am free, albeit for a moment. God give me the serenity to accept the things I can change. Man is born free, yet everywhere he goes he walks in chains (Rousseau). Give me the wisdom to know what I can change. Man can exist without an illusion, but the moment he parts with his dreams he ceases to live (M. Twain).

We've decided to seek the refuge of air conditioning. Our headlights point towards the Atlanta Aquarium. Hermes likes this idea; he adds that it might cheer me up. Grandpa is in wallet-related shock when he learns the price of admission. I seize the moment as I know that retreating would mean hours of frustration, disappointment, bickering, decision making, and map confusion. I place the ante into the computerized machines, our tickets spit out in similar disgust. Three hours of exploration, ooh's and ahh's from grandpa and the boys. Steph and I take pictures of our wards, of which grandpa appears to be one of them on this stop. Atlanta is the zenith of our excursion. From the museum we would point our toes north and make a circuitous route home. Halfway done is halfway empty. Halfway empty connotes experience behind and before us.

Our path leads us to Cloudland Canyons State Park in northwest Georgia. The route is rural with small plots of tobacco and okra. Gourd's hang aloft in yards serving as birdhouses. Small private oil drills pock the countryside. A flock of turkeys, I take note that they are markedly smaller than their northern cousins. The road becomes windy. I have a tailgater. Yet, I nimbly own each curve with only a few touchdowns of my foot-pedal. We register at the campground and I take my best stab at my southern accent and jokes with the workers. They graciously interact with me, laughing at my knee-slaps. We take a wrong turn or two within the campground. Finding our campground we setup camp in record time. We're close to the playground and take turns watching the boys frolic carelessly, the privilege of youth.

Hotdogs and marshmallows for supper. Hermes and I tend the fire and regret not having more time and resources…to travel more thoroughly… to take a break from the mundane, until a new mundane is created. Hermes and I own the night. We are lit by the effervescence of two citronella candles, one half full, the other half empty. I've never really cared too much about the half-empty or full paradigm. My line of questioning begs, what is the stuff made of, who is holding it, what is its purpose? No one knows. No one really knows what happens during the instant between freezing and thawing of water. We know so little, yet have the hubris to be so self-assured.

NORTH TO GETTYSBURG

August 12, 2011

Dear Joe and Rosa,

Today was another hot scorcher: Over 105 degrees! I jumped ship today with the gypsy-carnies and have joined a groovy-peace loving hippy bus... I know, far out right!?

We started out today in the Great Smokey Mountains, on to Atlanta, Georgia. Now we've parked at Cloudland Canyon State Park, strumming our guitars to James Taylor covers, John Denver, and Beatles' tracks... "all we are saying...is give PEACE a chance".

Forever Yours,

Hermes

Silent moments of unmoving fill our night and wee hours as Hermes and I communicate on a plane or frequency shared by very few, very infrequently. It is well enough to just be. To just exist. Still, at times we are almost combative in our verse. At times we leave this sphere and battle in high and low places. Places where legions of demons and angels gather around us, switching sides in an instant. Yet we don't know what we are fighting for or why. Oh! To be status quo…to sleep in the sweet nectar of common acceptance! It's a fanciful dream. Once a person has eaten from the tree of knowledge, they can never return to more Elysian fields. One is doomed to a fate of questions. After all, education is the path from cocky ignorance to miserable uncertainty-M. Twain.

In a fit of tossing and turning and tuning out, sleep captured me and owned me for five fleeting hours. I awoke to the sound of my body rustling the blue tarp below me. Grandpa and the boys went for a walk. The fire is out. I set to rebuilding it with little luck. Runny eggs and burnt toast was our fare, and everyone attempted to swallow it with grace.

Out of sync with our original itinerary, we pass the resolution to forge ahead to Mammoth Caves. I will forego the Cherokee Trail as we have lost a day and a half. Our budget is shrinking, yet still manageable. The northern road from Cloudland Canyons is a series of steep windy switchbacks. Fifteen mph warning signs go unheeded as we race down the mountain at a frightening clip, of which my foot pedal landed on more than one hairpin turn. Into Chattanooga I'm saluting fellow bikers as we parallel this awesome and wide slow moving river.

We cross an enormous bridge and cool air drifts up giving me some reprieve. Next a dam structure. We are on the Cherokee Trail for a few minutes, passing the Cherokee Trail Removal Museum. My heart sinks and separates in disparate directions. Our nation cannot exist upon such a faulty foundation as its genocide of Natives forever. Tom's leading at a hoary speed, I cannot pull over.

Entering Kentucky we find majestic mansions with miles of white wooden horse fences. Miles upon miles of corn and tobacco! Such a different experience than the small time producers of northwest Georgia; all things exist in contrast. Without contrast there is no existence. I see the duality in all things. To many of the Iroquois, George Washington was a rapacious liar. To the British he was a treasonous felon, and to us he has attained saintly status as our official first president of the United States of America. There were actually six presidents of the Continental Congress before him, not sure why they never made it into the history books?

Duality exists in all things, we learn by contrasts. Words that beckon me to the dark night of my soul, I shrug and contort my helmet covered head. It's a very long ride, grandpa is finally catching on to the boys' beverage tryst. The car smells horrendous and has not been cleaned since McGraw! Soda bottles, empty snack packages, squished and half eaten food radiates an oafish aroma. It's unbearable for me to reach into the car, I don't know how they ride for hours like this.

After eight or so hours on the road we near the Mammoth Caves region. The clouds open and rain blankets us in a deluge. Hard and strong and it's over. There is no vacancy in the national park. We stumble upon Diamond Caves resort. The office is abandoned, however there are directions to set up camp across the road and register the following morning. Tom didn't see this sign, score one for me. We travel across the road to a wonderful campground. Drenched like a drowned rat I follow Tom as we decide, re-decide, and finally decide on one campsite. We camp on an outer loop yet near the latrine and washer-dryer. I take a break from setting up camp and park it on a picnic bench. I tip the bench over and land on my back, very amusing to everyone but me.

LIBERTY

August 13, 2011

Dear Joe and Rosa,

Here are pictures from the Atlanta Aquarium. I met Patrick Starr from *SpongeBob* fame! I had my picture taken with an aquarium girl, swam with sharks, chatted with penguins, and overall had a great time! Oh, here are two pictures of the Smokey Mountains too!

Have you ever noticed that life is always moving? Everyday, time, change…its all part of the constant flow of life. Yet, life can be very still, static or unchanging. Take five minutes to sit still, no talking, no thinking, no-thing…Eternity is in the now. Seize the day! Because now is all we have.

Forever Yours,

Hermes

Songs: *Underpressure,* **David Bowie**

People are People, **Depeche Mode**

The campground hosts a large playground and swimming pool. Of which we enjoy both as Stephanie launders our rank garb. Later Tom and I clean out the car and cannot find the one major culprit of the distinct smell. We haphazardly toss in car fresheners, doesn't help much. Another night's vigil with Hermes, there is no penetrating thought that lingers. A complacent mirth fills our souls as we muse along happy and thankful lines. Mammoth Caves was a phenomenal experience for all of us. We enjoyed the tour.

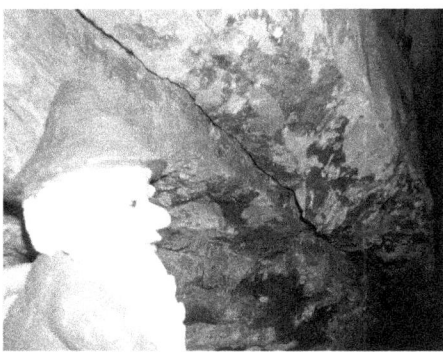

William and Haydn hiked the two and a quarter miles by themselves. At the end of the tour there was a towering steel stairwell that climbed over 200 vertical feet. This scared me. I felt pretty claustrophobic. Tom and Steph enjoyed innocent ribbing at my expense regarding one section of the caves called fat man's misery. Of which, I happily play along knowing that banter is fun and payback is a bitch.

August 15, 2011

Dear Joe and Rosa,

Still in the South. I've seen acres and acres of tobacco plants, southern plantations, and wide-slow flowing rivers like the Kentucky River. People are very charming here until you tell them that you are from New York. It's gotta be our pizza!

On another level, I've been pondering the ageless question: Why do bad things happen? Many religions contend that we chose our hardships or that the trials of life make us stronger. I don't know, sounds too weak or anemic; not a real answer. I've found that there are no guarantees in life, that all things "good" come with a "bad" corollary; duality in all things.

Many musical influences have trickled through my gnome noggin today:

Civil War, Guns & Roses; *Black & White, Shambala,* Three Dog Night; *I Am I Said,* Neil Diamond; *I Am That I Am,* Peter Tosh; *War,* by Edwin Starr; *Backstabbers,* The O'Jays; and *You Were On My Mind,* We Five.

Forever Yours,

Hermes

Another day of driving lay ahead of us. No rest for the wicked. We entered West Virginia via an expansive bridge that covered an enormous swath of water. A nuclear plant is nestled away amongst the mountains to the left, their stacks billowing profusely emitting wide columns of smoke that break up the otherwise riparian countryside. It rains. The rain is cold and coming down in sheets and often sideways. For the next five hours I bend over Spirit's gas tank. At times we slow down to 30 mph, water cannot travel off the windy mountainous roads fast enough. There is a constant four or five inch stream of water on the road, nasty conditions for riding bike. This is the life I chose, Live to ride, ride to live. Much to others' amusement and my chagrin people pass me with a smirk. *I'll give you something to smirk about,* I say wryly aloud to myself.

All throughout West Virginia it rained. When we pulled over about five p.m., I was chilled to the bone. I stood outside in the pouring rain as Tom asked the innkeeper for a room, sorry no room nor manger here. We travel another forty miles or so and ask the same, we are invited in and I am most grateful.

Steph and I do the dance in our hotel room. The kids are there watching us, listening. We are arguing about money, nothing new neither for us nor for husbands and wives throughout time immemorial. I am a minority. In many ways I am a statistical minority…according to Title 9 legislation I am anything but a minority. Title 9 is a piece of legislation that insures equality, due process, and protection for women and ethnic minorities. Title 9 is a huge funding source that balloons out and influences small business grant and loan policies, hiring and firing, and state or federal oversight agencies. Which is well and good. However, Title 9 makes the fallacious assumption that white men are born with either a silver spoon in their mouths or an ala carte' boon of opportunities that organically unfold before them.

I might propose that proponents of the mythical white male privilege read *The Beans of Egypt, Maine* by Carolyn Chute. Chute paints a picture more typical of the rural white male than is commonly believed in the privileged white male myth. My sophomore English teacher prodded me to read this book in high school. Be careful as you read this book, because your life will change. If you're one to quip "I don't know why people just don't pull themselves up by their bootstraps," than this tome will be a challenge for you. There are people in urban and rural America, black, white, yellow and brown that do not have bootstraps nor boots, period.

White men have financial and vocational difficulties too! The breakdown is: Black women, Hispanic women, black men, white women and finally white men that statistically are economically challenged. Not all white men are Rockefellers or Kennedys. The landscape of America's workplace is changing…if ever so slowly, in the right direction. I would never disparage or begrudge women's rights. However, I define equality in work and home as a willingness and ability to juxtaposition traditional roles and chores. If men were responsible for automobile and yard upkeep women should be willing to rise from under that yoke. The same should hold true for men with respect to childrearing and housekeeping.

Research is showing that women are not getting the better end of the stick. Women are working outside of the homes, statistically being paid about 15% less than men for comparable work and with slower advancement opportunities while still shouldering most of the domestic duties.

Are women winning? Meh. What happens if a family opts to have a single income family? Are single income families comparable in financial lifestyle to dual income families? In our ever-increasing consumption society, single income families pay a price, and dual income families pay another price. Single income families often find themselves at the poverty line, going with out vacations, extra curricular activities and enrichment, and shopping for less healthy products at less than optimal stores.

Dual income families never seem to leave the hustle and bustle of their careers. Others raise their children, and children often have little respect for their parents and an insatiable appetite for things. Absentee career parents often attempt to compensate for their A.W.O.L. status through store bought bribes. These bribes are social status symbols to reassure themselves, and their kids, their neighbors that work pays. Erstwhile, children are existing in a whirlpool of divorce, other baby daddies, and little affection. The art and science of family is disappearing at an alarming rate from our social panorama. Never before in history have life's foundation or building blocks eroded so quickly. We really don't know the results of this fast tempoed direction.

Steph wants me to be the chef, the baker, and the candlestick maker. She wants me to do all the housework, yard work, and bring in the lion's share of money. However, she has not really carved out her role. She is short and curt with the boys. She is lost as to when and how to discipline them. She comes from a hoarding background. Living in a rat's nest is comfortable for her, it's foreign for her to exist in a clean or semi-clean environment. I love her. I want her to be happy yet there is an insurmountable schism here that will separate us forever. We both shirk each other and the topic of money off with a whatever.

I sleep sans protest or vigil. One more stop, it's the last leg of our journey, and I am at peace. I realize that all good things must end. We are headed to Gettysburg. Stephanie and William are Civil War buffs. Hopefully this will be a special treat for them both especially after visiting the Lincoln Memorial and following the path of much of the war. Round Top campgrounds is at the opposite corner of Gettysburg of which we came in on. We travel through Gettysburg. Round Top Campground greets us with a working waterwheel and koi pond. The office seconds as a camp store with a swimming pool off to the left through double doors.

Our tent campsite appears to be the backyard of an adjacent housing division. We return to the camp office and ask for an upgrade, something with a few trees and not in the neighbor's back yard. We finally grab a campsite not far from the main facilities. We will stay here two nights enjoying the pool, cooking over the fire and seeing the sites.

Tom and I both witnessed a wardrobe malfunction of an attractive mom in the swimming pool. It feels good to be off the road. I cook mash potatoes and pork chops over the fire. The Gettysburg memorial is a treat. We are in awe as the cyclorama brings the war to life before us. I had forgotten that Gettysburg was pivotal in the war for two reasons: 1. It was a day's march away from Harrisburg the state capitol. Had the confederates conquered so far north, many of the northern supporters across the seas would jump ship. 2. Gettysburg was a virtual hub with spokes of roads traveling in all directions, and it would have been impossible to halt confederate supply chains had we lost this diminutive town. Liberty hung in the balance, and barely lived to tell the story.

I have budgeted a few trinkets for the boys at this historic site. I mail the last of Hermes epistles. The future lies before us. We roast the last hot dogs and s'mores on our last night camping, and the end of our journey lies before us. Tomorrow would find us home. It is all too anti-climatic. However, I know that I have changed. I have come to terms with some of the specters that lie in the mists and shadows of higher thought.

LIBERTY

Candybars Kill Democracy

I tapped away at the keyboard in a dank closet dwarfed by musky English literature books from the 1960's. My office was located at the end of a hallway; a dead-end, much like the future of the at-risk teenagers that I worked with. Unbeknownst to me, my stetorious career would dead-end in that office. The death of my soul lurked in that dark crevasse; I just didn't know it yet.

The principal's voice flitted over the P.A. system, announcing a competition to raise money for the local food pantry. I slinked out of my cavern, the proverbial critter slithering out from under its stone. I hailed my neighbor, a jovial and much liked underclass Civics instructor, and inquired about this competition. He replied with a smile from his slouch that he has a long history of *attempting* to win the most money for the food pantry, and this year as an added bonus he would get to wear the greatly vied for turkey costume.

I sized up my colleague, and mentally weighed him for the ability to win such a race. Aside from donning a man-girdle, I thought he was a shoe-in for the race. He just needed a campaign manager. Someone with zest, creativity, and a passion for food pantry cooked turkey costumes. I was the man for the job, he was the bird for the outfit, together we would kick some tail.

Through the labyrinth of school hallways lurked a greater enemy, something dark, a macabre twist that would snatch the much vied for turkey costume from our claws. New to the school was a young svelte assistant principal. The powers that be pinned him, the towering young administrator, as the champion for the race. The die was cast, we had lost before we begun… a part of democracy died that day, and so did a part of me.

Tyranny nearly always starts with a lie, a tryst, and a raging groundswell of applause. The lie is grounded in pleas: Pleas of hope, of change, of equality, and greater levels of service. The lie is framed in fear. Fear is the proverbial stick that drives the bovine-like masses in a direction, and often off a cliff. There are lies and liars.

The tryst is a devil's agreement whispered in shadowy closets where one hand washes the other, yet everyone remains dirty. In the case of the foul fowl race, on this particular stage in life stood a promising young school administrator, a senior class Government teacher/advisor. On stage left stood the entire student body, faculty, staff, a group of six at-risk students, and myself. And between these two disparate groups stood a mountain of candy bars.

The competition was to raise the most money for a food pantry. The lie was, there would be an equitable and honorable level playing ground. The tryst involved a candy bar store located in the Senior Government teacher's room that only seniors had access to. The big boys on campus decided that the seniors would vote in block, all at once with their candy bar money. What happened here happens everywhere… the haves dupe the masses… whilst disproportionately monopolizing the resources of power. No amount of grass-roots effort would turn the tide. Seniors had part-time jobs compared to their economically disadvantaged underclass counterparts. Seniors had sole access to this store. The seniors came out in full-force in modern day e-bay force. Namely, holding on to the bulk of their funds until the last fifteen minutes of the competition, further duping the masses that they had a chance to win.

I saw the senior Government/advisor in the hallway the next day. No words were spoken. However a moment of knowing recognition passed between us. She had known, and I had known what had happened. It's doubtful that anyone else shared our knowledge. The Government teacher's secret was safe with me. Her secret would have been drowned out by a quick succession of school festivities, a roaring applause. I felt this experience deeply on many levels.

To wear a turkey costume is one thing… after all, democracy, equality, and justice can be second ranked behind a turkey costume and money for the food bank. At one level the jejune and naïve underclassmen were inculcated to American democracy, however latent and subconscious. Watching these young and malleable students fall for the dummy game was sad.

The part of me that died was seeing the comparison in the real world. The year before this incident I had spoken with a nominating committee for a state assemblyman race. I thought I had a lot of knowledge, passion and hard work that I could add to the communal soup as a State Assemblymen. My findings showed that I was too impoverished to run a race for the low, albeit important office of state assemblyman.

More importantly, I mourned over the souls and lives of the six at-risk students that I worked with. They were all too bright for their own britches. These students had lived through horrendous environmental circumstances. They had championed personal demons each day and most had excelled academically. They were referred to me for basically not fitting in. They were too rebellious to fellow teachers, staff and students. I had spent a great amount of time with them as their greatest cheerleader. You can do it! You are smart! You are brave! You are great! You are loved!

I guess I hit four out of five with my efforts. Honestly, they can't do it. They are not supposed to do it. They are supposed to put up with it gracefully. Statistically, they will be what they are, poor, unrepresentative and minions to a higher order, a greater caste.

My failure with these students goes deeper. My employment was through a non-profit organization outside of the school district. I was placed in the school as a form of subcontracted position. My direct boss had problems. I had problems. Our problems were problematic.

My youngest son developed e-coli symptoms. There was an outbreak within peanut butter snack crackers that might have caused this illness. He was not keeping food down, he had a fever of a 103 degrees, and had diarrhea. These symptoms made him lose weight drastically. He was labeled failure to thrive, with no end in sight to the symptoms. I took a week off to be with him, nurture him, and do anything in my power to make him well. We thought he could die.

My boss called me after receiving our doctor's note. "How dare you take a week off from work, this is very unprofessional." She followed along these lines in a disparaging tone for nearly an hour, while I had my sick son on my hip getting sick. No amount of diplomacy would dissuade her from her unidentified objective. Finally my wife came home and I whispered around the phone as to whom it was, what was going on, how long I had been on the phone. We concluded that I should make a summative statement, apologize, let my boss know that I had to go, announce that I was going now. And hang up. My boss didn't like that.

Not to disparage others' ways of life, but she is one of these people you meet that have no kids. Rather, they have faithful dogs that they put in kennels for their trips out of town, vacations etc. Her experience as a parent and all that parenthood entails never developed. The problems deepened with her. She was very fickle in her policies. She was unreliable in her advice. She showed up to group supervision meetings with inappropriate attire, more night-clubish than work-a-day garb. Other colleagues noticed this. The secretaries at our main office had cautionary tales of this supervisor going through six employees in less than 12 months. The writing was on the wall.

We were to report our caseload progress to her after hours. I was traveling to meet her alone in empty office space when I stopped to fuel up. One of my colleagues was gassing up as well. "Hey, did you hear the news?" what news? "Our boss filed sexual harassment on her boss." How did you hear about this? "She told me." Clink... I stopped fueling up and my jaw dropped. Lord have mercy on our boss' boss if he acted inappropriately. However, with the mounting list of unprofessional behavior exhibited by my boss, I thought it prudent to meet with her after all of this messy business was cleared up. She didn't like this. Nor did she apologize for circumventing the internal and legal process to protect her boss' privacy should the internal investigation exonerate him.

By this time I had made an indelible difference in my caseload's life. Anger issues were down, grades were up, detention referrals down, parent-teacher-school administrator approval for the students and the program had sky rocketed. In the words of one skeptic and reticent to teacher, "I didn't believe in the counseling program or process until you showed up. Your dedication to these kids has made all the difference." This teacher originally didn't even want me in her classroom. At the end of my tenure she was one of the students' biggest supporters.

I compiled and filed a chronology of concerns regarding my direct supervisor, along with "testimonials" and references from within my school placement, regarding the work that I was performing. The non-profit organization that I represented did not want to do anything with this wayward supervisor. They turned her loose and she was attempting to undo all of the work that I had done in all the clever ways of a lonely sadist. I tendered my resignation hoping for a school counseling position within the district that I was placed at.

What I failed to understand is: That school district had not employed a male counselor in the past twenty-five years. Ten positions had been vacated, filled, vacated and filled again over twenty-five years time without one male representative. This school district sat at an affordable crossroads to multiple private and state counselor preparation programs. My heart sank, I was screwed. I felt betrayed. I retreated to a nearby national forest and pleaded with God for guidance, for support, for comfort, much as I did in my youth. I entered a profound forest of sadness of which I have never returned. I prayed, I believed, I died.

I pray to God that the hoary scenes of the Luray grave will never haunt me again. Not sure if this is yet another prayer that seemingly falls upon deaf ears. That night in the campground, the last night of our journey, as I closed my eyes and drifted off to sleep, I am faced with my worst nightmare. I am standing before an old oak tree, one that I knew well. This oak tree stood in front of my Stanley home. My first home. All my life I prayed for a home, a family… the status quo. I fought against the current for fifteen years serving at-risk children and their families. It was here at this tree that I lost my soul. Here amongst the roots lies a part of me that will never live again. I knelt and prayed here. I prayed for the souls of the children I was working with, I prayed for deliverance from the surreal world that I was forced to wander through. I prayed for my sons. I prayed for my wife.

I believe that effort is the first step on the path to failure.

I believe that some people will always get their pound of flesh, don't fight it.

LIBERTY

God's Grace, White "T's", And The Voices In My Head

No matter what I had done in my life, it had never been enough to bring down God's grace in my life. No amount of faith or works would be enough to save my soul. And here in the middle of the night as I fitfully slumbered over Lincoln's hallowed ground I saw my own grave, the resting place of the best part of my soul. This part of my soul believed in mankind. Believed in fighting for a higher purpose. Believed in prayer, and in a compassionate and engaged God that would be there.

We lost our home, like so many people of this time. It's over, I lost my sanity here. I became suicidal. Tom and my mom would rent a truck, we left in a weekend. My family stayed in their unfinished basement. Thanksgiving and Christmas would be a death march for me. We slept on air mattresses. During the day I stared at the pink insulation falling from the ceiling. Straight and true pipes hung above me. Stephanie would find us a leaky abandoned trailer to rent. Medications and therapy have done little to assuage the profound spiritual death and rejection that I have earned. I am numb. I am dead inside.

There is very little solace to be found. I know that I am not alone in the way that I think and react to the pressures of our society. Many people lost their homes with the housing crisis of 2008. Many people can relate to the angst that I feel regarding livable wages, and the unrealized democracy that America attempts to boast of having. What is to be done? What is the next chapter in our troubled nation? Our troubles have nearly reached the boiling point. Mankind will not be held under the oppressive yolk of tyranny without revolting.

Many people look to apocrophal texts to illuminate and understand what is or will happen in the latter days of mans existence. People refer to the writings of Nostrodomas or the calendar of the Mayan's to guide their way. The field is rife with interpreters and interpretations of what these dusty tomes speak to our modern times.

I believe that the current generation is similitude to the White Horseman described in Revelations 19:15-16. This era, this demography that profusely colludes with what I have written about here could be interpreted as the White Horseman identified in Revelations nineteen. The Orthodox Hebrew men that I met in a state park earlier on in this journey read the writing aloud that was written upon my t-shirt and thigh: "King of Kings, and Lord of Lords." Without question, I do not profess to be a messiah figure, nor an angel nor a daemon. However, I count myself as part of this new era, this demography that demands a new movement, a greater commitment to democratic principles, and end to our failed system of governance, unrealized democracy, and irresponsible capitalism.

I may not know who or what "The King of Kings, and Lord of Lords" is. However I do know that it is not found or connected with our current ways of doing things as a nation. These are the voices in my head. These are the spectors that haunt me like Pirsig's Phaedrus. The voices in my head beckon across space and time demanding of me, to lift up this herald, to finish the work that they have begun. That no woman or man should exist with the lies and corruption spoon fed to them by today's leadership.

LIBERTY

August 17, 2011

Dear Joe and Rosa,

I stopped and visited my Confederate-Rebel cousin Shermes, Sherm for short. People always picked on him in school changing his "h" for a "p", not funny, poor guy! Anywhoo, I've learned a lot out here on the road. I'm more o.k. with myself and the world.

My hippy-biker friends and I were hanging out in a hotel the other night. On the telly was The Wizard of Oz. And everything fell into place; No matter what life throws at you, no matter how hard life gets…

It *really* is true…
There really is
No place like…
Gnome!!!

Forever Yours,

Hermes

See you real soon.

MH Kisner

Hermes Returns Home

The ride home was very anti-climatic. Not a cloud in the sky. The warmth of mid-August heat enveloped us as we pressed northward. Very little was said, and even more sparse were thoughts. Thoughts seemed to evaporated like morning dew, blown this way and that way like the now absent clouds.

We were surrounded by what is, and I was ok with it. To atone for my miscreant and thieving behavior, Hermes and I purchased a basket of thoughtful and sweet gifts. Hermes sat in a basket, garnished by chocolates, coffee mugs, snacks, candles and other treats. Not sure what treatment Hermes and I would endure, we brought grandpa with us to assuage any hurt feelings inflicted by wayward garden gnomes and bikers.

We returned from whence we came; The Fairlane 50's diner in Mc-Graw, NY. Joe and Rosa greeted us in spite of being robbed of one of their favorite pals of the garden variety. The conversation was instantly warm and booming as Rosa, dressed as Lucille Ball with her mighty husband in miniature greeted us with: We thought it was you! We didn't know who was sending letters! What is this all about? Wide natural smiles of close friends and family garnished every patron's face in the diner.

Self-consciously, I confessed to my nearly botched theft. We talked at length about the letters, pictures and post cards that I sent home. It was more than a little awkward to explain why Hermes and I had to make a trip together. There were secrets that Hermes and I shared, which very few people will ever hear, see or experience.

The boys ordered their normal fare; hotdogs and grilled cheese and root beer. Tom followed suit with a burger. I went for a bowl of soup and a spectacular roast beef with horseradish melt. The conversation flitted back and forth from our adventures, the unique sites we saw, to more of the pedestrian "What routes did you take? How was the weather? Tell us about the people..." I was so happy to be off the hook. Hermes and I did not want to raise Rosa's and Joe's ire. We did not want to rock the boat, create a grudge or otherwise disenfranchise these fine people.

I anted up and paid the bill, and left a robust tip. I added, "Joe, it's in part for putting up with my shenanigans." Of which Joe and Rosa were gracious participants. Spirit was parked out front, visible through the semi-transparent effigy of Elvis. I could feel Spirit pulling me. The affection between biker and bike has no bounds. No wall or window can separate one's affection for their ride.

My attention drifted from Joe to Spirit. Eerily as ever, as I have never gotten used to it: Music floated in the air, drowning out Joe's words. His lips moved yet I could hear naught. Strumming from An acoustic guitar floated like on angel's wings and touched me. ... *tell me where is sanity?...tax the rich, feed the poor, 'till there are no rich no more.* My feet left the diner with Joe in-tow, still talking, probably inquiring more about our road trip.

I'd like to change the world...but I don't know what to do. I REALLY HAVE TO FIX THAT! I interject maybe a little too loud as I noticed Joe's physical reaction to nearly being shouted at over the music. Fix what? Joe probes. THAT!!! I am pointing at the bike, THE MUSIC JUST COMES ON OUT OF NOWHERE, I return in a loud boom still fighting with the music. What music? I don't hear music? Joe looks puzzled. *I'd love to change the world, but I don't know what to do...* The song eerily ends, just like how it began. I toss my helmet on my head, over my do rag. Now I am puzzled... I voice aloud through my helmet "Hmmpfff, maybe it's all in my head." I leave Joe.

Bibliography

Devol, P.E, Payne. Krabill, D.L., (2002). *Hidden rules of class at work.* Aha Process: Highlands Texas.

Devol, P.E, Payne, R.K., & Smith, T.D., (2006) *Bridges out of poverty: Strategies for professionals and communities workbook.* Aha Process: Highlands Texas.

Ehrenreich, B., (2001). *Nickel and Dimed: On not getting by in America.* Metropolitan Books: New York.

Ehrenreich, B., (2008). *This land is Their Land.* Metropolitan Books: New York.

Lubin, G., (Sept. 27, 2010). *10 signs the U.S. is losing its influence in the Western Hemisphere.* http://finance.yahoo.com

McWhinney, J.E., (2010). *6 signs that you've made it to middle class.* Http://finance.yahoo.com/news/6-signs-that-you've-made-it-to-investopedia-4243472351.html?x=0

Phillips, L., Garrett, E.M., (2010). *Why don't they just get a job? One couple's mission to end poverty in their community.* Aha Process: Highlands Texas.

Shipler, David. K., (2004). *The working poor: Invisible in America.* Alfred A. Knopf: New York.

Shulman, B., (2003) *The betrayal of work: How low-wage jobs fail 30 million Americans.* The New Press: New York.

Wang, A., & Wheatley, A.; editing by Wills, K., (Sept. 9, 2010). U.S. slips in WEF's competitiveness rankings. Http://news.yahoo.com

Yen, H., (2010). Census: *1 in 7 Americans live in poverty.* Http://news.yahoo.com/s/ap/20100916/ap_bi_ge/us_census_poverty

Yen, H., (2010). *Census finds record gap between rich and poor.* Http://news.yahoo.com/s/ap/20100928/ap_bi_ge/us_census_poverty

www.ingramcontent.com/pod-product-compliance
Lightning Source LLC
Chambersburg PA
CBHW061443040426
42450CB00007B/1191